SNOWSHOEING

OUTDOOR PURSUITS SERIES

Sally Edwards
Melissa McKenzie

Human Kinetics

D0060447

Library of Congress Cataloging-in-Publication Data

Edwards, Sally, 1947-
   Snowshoeing / Sally Edwards, Melissa McKenzie.
      p.   cm. -- (Outdoor pursuits series)
   Includes index.
   ISBN 0-87322-767-0
   1. Snowshoes and snowshoeing. I. McKenzie, Melissa, 1955- .
II. Title. III. Series.
GV853.E38   1995
796.92--dc20   94-40482
                                                                        CIP

ISBN: 0-87322-767-0

Photos on pages 2, 26, 52, and 105 © Rob Bossi, Portsmouth, NH.
Photos on pages 36 – 38, 40 – 44, 54, 65, and 121 © Roy Wilcox.

Series Editor and Developmental Editor: Holly Gilly; **Assistant Editors:** Julie Marx Ohnemus, Dawn Roselund, Kirby Mittelmeier; **Copyeditor:** John Wentworth; **Proofreader:** Anne Meyer Byler; **Typesetters:** Stuart Cartwright, Ruby Zimmerman; **Text Designer:** Keith Blomberg; **Layout Artist:** Stuart Cartwright; **Photo Editor:** Karen Maier; **Cover Designer:** Jack Davis; **Interior Art:** Thomas • Bradley Illustration and Design; **Cover Photo:** John Kelly; **Printer:** Buxton Skinner

Human Kinetics books are available at special discounts for bulk purchase. Special editions or book excerpts can also be created to specification. For details, contact the Special Sales Manager at Human Kinetics.

Printed in the United States of America   10 9 8 7 6 5 4 3 2 1

Human Kinetics
P.O. Box 5076, Champaign, IL 61825-5076
1-800-747-4457

Canada: Human Kinetics, Box 24040, Windsor, ON N8Y 4Y9
1-800-465-7301 (in Canada only)

Europe: Human Kinetics, P.O. Box IW14, Leeds LS16 6TR, England
(44) 532 781708

Australia: Human Kinetics, 2 Ingrid Street, Clapham 5062, South Australia
(08) 371 3755

New Zealand: Human Kinetics, P.O. Box 105-231, Auckland 1
(09) 309 2259

CONTENTS

1

GOING
SNOW-
SHOEING

When was the last time you did something for the first time? Stop and ask yourself that question. It is imposing. It is challenging. It is one of the reasons we snowshoe. We asked ourselves this question one winter morning in 1991. Once we decided it had been too long since our last "first time," we were off to pursue a mutual first that we had been curious about for some time—snowshoeing. We made halting progress, however, because we didn't know where to go, what to take, what to do, or, for that matter, what wild critters awaited us—basically, we knew nothing about the sport or how to get started.

But somehow we did get started, and our first snowshoeing experience changed our lives. That morning, we packed a lunch and headed to the

Sierra Nevadas. It was a blast. Our dogs couldn't have been happier, and when we stopped for a picnic lunch on the ridge line, we had a panoramic view of the western slopes of the Sierras. That was the defining moment in which we knew we had found a sport that could offer a blend of adventure, solitude, and peacefulness (and almost no learning curve!). We had to tell others about our discovery.

© R. Bossi

A sport fit for both the two- and four-legged crowd.

Since then there has been no looking back. In our snowshoes we have witnessed the winter world opening to us, as it will for you. Ultimately the act of snowshoeing can bring you so much: the thrills of the downhill, the joy of the silence, and the health and spiritual benefits that come from exploring the outdoors.

Getting Started on the Right Foot

Imagine yourself snowshoeing. Draw the mental picture. It looks like you, dressed warmly, wearing lightweight, easy-to-use snowshoes. It looks like you, walking with friends on your favorite summer trails, but this is terrain you can't cover in the summer because it doesn't exist then—this is a landscape that appears only in the winter, with its snow-white drifts and fields, and the only way to explore it is on snowshoes. It looks like you, doing a snowshoe run for fitness. It looks like you, discovering the tracks of a snowshoe hare. It looks like you, climbing up and out of your everyday routine and onto the nearest mountaintop.

Pretty picture, isn't it? Now that you are done imagining it, get out and do it. Grab a friend, a pair of shoes, your gear, and go.

We grabbed quite a few friends one night last winter, when we decided to invite a group to join us on a "winter wandering about" adventure—a full-moon snowshoe walk. We asked several dozen people, assuming only a few would show up. It was a pleasant shock when we arrived at the Nordic resort we were starting from and found a crowd of 65 waiting for us—only 2 of whom had ever shoed before. The ski resort folks had built a bonfire in the middle of a meadow; it would be a relaxed, 45-minute walk to our destination.

We sensed in our companions a nervous excitement blending with their hunger for adventure. Bringing up the rear and pulling a sled loaded with marshmallows, graham crackers, and chocolate bars, we joined our friends at the bonfire and started to listen and talk. All present were asked to introduce and say one positive thing about themselves. We heard some say they were not sure why they had wanted to come, but they knew why now.

We returned to our homes close to midnight. Most of us had to be at work the next morning, but no one seemed tired. We shared a feeling of up-liftedness, much like a runner's high. Over the next several weeks, we received letters and phone calls from the moonlight snowshoers saying how much they had appreciated our invitation. Their comments ranged from "I really needed the hike—it helped me find something inside myself" to "Why didn't anyone ever tell me that winter could be so much fun?" For us, we had simply wanted to share with others the joy of winter wandering about. We didn't know the impact it would have. But now we do.

The snowshoeing experience can be simple, with minimal preparation and training, as you've seen from our moonlight walk, but somehow its rewards far outweigh the investment. Read on. Then you too can join us floating on the snow.

SNOWSHOEING THROUGH TIME

Snowshoes arrived in North America from Central Asia some 6,000 years ago, at a time when the Bering Strait was passable by foot. The indigenous people of North America were the first great snowshoe designers. Starting with a basic bearpaw shape, they developed hundreds of frame patterns suited to all possible snow and terrain conditions.

When the first Europeans arrived in North America, they adopted the snowshoe. During the European expansion snowshoes were very helpful to trappers, hunters, explorers, and surveyors, particularly in Canada.

In the mid-1800s, snowshoe clubs began organizing the first snowshoe races, with distances ranging from 100 yards (91 m) to 6 miles (9.7 km). These clubs also organized snowshoe "tramps," or training workouts. Other early snowshoe events grew in popularity as well; Canadian winter carnivals and New England community snowshoe hikes thrived through the late 1930s.

It wasn't until 1862 in Maine that the first commercial, large-scale production of snowshoes began. Other manufacturers joined in, and after only a few decades the majority of snowshoes were factory built. Still, it wasn't until the 1950s and the development of Western snowshoes (as sport snowshoes were originally known) that the modern era in snowshoeing began.

A Type of Snowshoeing for You

The basic snowshoe concept—staying aloft by increasing the surface area of your feet, thereby reducing how much you sink in the snow—is pretty unsophisticated. Snowshoes are basically foot extenders. But the development of snowshoes as a means of travel ranks up there with the invention of the wheel—and snowshoes can take you where wheels cannot.

Yet, when people think of snowshoeing they typically visualize someone trudging along with rough-hewn tennis rackets strapped to her feet. Quaint, but most fitness and recreational athletes would find such a workout unappealing. Fortunately, any notions of snowshoeing as laborious and primitive no longer have basis in fact. Thanks to ever-improving technology and design, today's sport snowshoes are light, stylish, and fun. They have turned the drudgery of the past into the revolutionary new pastime of today.

© F-Stock/David Stoecklein

Snowshoeing no longer means trudging through the snow with tennis rackets strapped to your feet.

Today's snowshoers take advantage of the new lighter and slimmer sport snowshoes to race, hike, and explore areas previously off limits to all but the most intrepid or unwary. Whether it's a long stretch of wilderness or your own backyard, modern sport snowshoes allow you to go where you want to go, in style and comfort.

Still not sure that snowshoeing is for you? Well, there happen to be snowshoeing options to suit almost all tastes and abilities. The three basic types of sport snowshoeing activities are walking and recreation, training and racing, and back-country mountaineering and winter camping. This book prepares you thoroughly for the first type and adequately for the second. If you get hooked on snowshoeing and want to do some camping or mountaineering, we recommend you pick up a couple of other books that go into greater detail about these more advanced activities. The appendix lists some good ones.

Remember that you don't need to be athletic or outdoorsy to have fun in the snow. In fact, if you are one of the millions of people who helped make exercise walking the hugely popular participation sport it is, then snow-shoeing may well be for you. Snowshoeing is the wintertime version of exercise walking. If you live outside the Sunbelt, you know that winter walking in your tennis shoes just won't do.

Do you think snowshoeing sounds too casual or sedate? If so, think again. At the 1993 Mt. Hood Snowshoe Race, runner Herb Lindsey, who once held the United States record in the 10,000 meters, overcame other competitive snowshoers to win the overall men's racing division. Four-time Olympic biathlete Lyle Nelson won the snowshoe/cross-country ski biathlon. Sport

© Carl Heilman II

Snowshoeing is fun for the young and the young at heart.

snowshoeing attracts athletes from other sports not only because it is simple to start right in but also because the physical effort one expends can be adjusted to suit the fitness needs of everyone, from novice to pro.

Maybe you're not interested in exercise for its own sake. Well, if you love the great outdoors, snowshoeing is the best way to experience all its winter glory. Hikers, trackers, campers, and mountaineers can all pick up and put on a pair of snowshoes at minimal expense and with little, if any, learning curve.

And how does snowshoeing stack up against skiing? When people ask us to compare snowshoeing with skiing, we say, "no contest." Here's why:

- *Snowshoeing is easy to learn.* You don't need lessons, because if you can walk, you can snowshoe. Age, sex, size, conditioning, and coordination are not factors.

- *Snowshoeing is inexpensive.* Once you have purchased the snowshoes, there are no other necessary expenses except transportation to and from the trailhead.

- *Snowshoeing is low- to no-maintenance.* With modern snowshoes, there's no waxing to worry about, and there is very little chance of equipment breakage.

- *Snowshoeing is convenient.* You don't need a packed trail to snowshoe. Snowshoes are also easier to carry in the field than skis are, in addition to being a breeze to transport to and from your destination.

- *Snowshoeing is safe.* The possibility of being injured while wearing snowshoes is slight, and the chances of falling on snowshoes are far less than on skis.

- *Snowshoeing is fast.* When you've got a direct destination, you can almost always go right to it; there are few long detours to get past the kind of obstructions that skis can't handle.

- *Snowshoeing is slow . . . when you want it to be.* Snowshoes allow you to take the time to explore your winter surroundings, to go off trail and spend half an hour tracking a fox if you want.

- *Snowshoeing goes with camping.* You can't beat snowshoes for winter backpacking (not to mention the fact that snowshoes are very efficient for stamping out a campsite).

- *Snowshoeing is good exercise.* Well, skiing is too, so let's just call it a draw on this one!

- *Snowshoeing is for anyone.* Wanderer, walker, cross-trainer, runner, racer, tracker, camper, climber, explorer—all of you, you'll love it.

So, are you a walker, hiker, racer, parent with active kids, outdoorsperson, or cross-trainer? Are you trying to get (or remain) fit, or do you simply enjoy being outdoors? If so, snowshoeing is for you. Read on and we'll show you how to get where you want to go and have a great time getting there.

In the following chapters you'll find a comprehensive guide to getting on the right snowy path and staying there. If you're looking for thorough instruction on snowshoeing, read the chapters in order. If you already have the basics down, use this book as a reference and consult the chapters, appendix, and index as needed. Of course, we think all readers can gain something from sharing our snowshoeing experiences. We hope doing so inspires you all to go out and have some snowshoeing experiences of your own!

MOONS AND MOTHERS

I have always loved the outdoors. Although I don't consider myself an athlete, I do like to keep fit. In summer I swim, hike, and climb mountains. In winter I cross-country ski. I had heard about snowshoeing and what a great way it is to experience the wilderness. Ten years ago, I rented a pair of the old-style heavy wooden frames laced with animal hides. Although the snow was beautiful and the day sparkling clear, the clumsy snowshoes destroyed what could have been a special experience. Not only did they feel as if they were falling off, they did fall off, repeatedly, until I simply gave up.

By the time I met Sally and Melissa, I was convinced that snowshoeing was not for me. However, when they invited me on a full-moon showshoe hike, I decided to give the newer, high-tech snowshoes a try. The night in the California Sierras was beautiful. Between clouds the moon created magic on the snow, and I felt truly part of nature. After a 2-mile (3.2-km) walk, we clustered around a campfire and shared stories. To enhance the mood, I read some quotations and poems.

Encouraged by our magic moonlight evening, and at Sally's suggestion, I decided to invite my mother for a daytime snowshoe walk.

Mother has always been adventurous. In her youth she was an avid hiker, climber, and swimmer. But at age 81, she has had to slow down. Although she was initially reluctant to try snowshoeing, I convinced her when I asked, "How many new things do you get to try at this point in your life?"

So we went back to the Sierras, and I fitted her with snowshoes and ski poles for stability. The day was just perfect, and the trail we chose was uncrowded. I would have been afraid to take Mother cross-country skiing because there is so much more to learn and the danger of falling is greater. But on snowshoes she felt perfectly stable, and we could adjust to her pace. When I asked her later what she liked about the day, she said, "I was thrilled to be able to walk on the snow without falling through. I was exhilarated with my new adventure. I loved the silence and the beauty of winter, and it was so nice to experience it without feeling crowded."

It was a special experience for us both. She is already asking me when we are going again. Thanks to the new generation of snowshoes, a snowy walk in the woods is a treat I can enjoy with friends of all ages.

—Marty Maskall

2

SNOW-
SHOEING
EQUIPMENT

You're right to think the first things you need to snowshoe are the shoes! But before you run out and pluck a pair off the shelf, we recommend that you learn a little bit about them. Once you've got the basics down—snowshoe components, different models, and so on—you'll be in a much better position to choose the right pair for you. After that, you can start thinking about the gear, clothing, and accessories that will complete your snowshoeing picture.

What Kind of Snowshoes Do You Need?

Thanks to ever-improving technology and the recent progression of snowshoes from back-country tool to sporting toy, there are now enough types of snowshoes available to suit anyone's tastes and needs. The various snowshoes you'll find on the market fall into two general categories: traditional snowshoes and sport snowshoes. Which kind is best for you depends on your intentions and habits.

The primary rule in determining the best snowshoe for you is to select the smallest and lightest weight snowshoe that provides the necessary flotation. The other thing to keep in mind is that in varying snow conditions, different

© Carl Heilman II

Traditional snowshoes are beautifully crafted.

shoes work best for different uses. This could lead the high-intensity shoer to make multiple purchases.

Traditional snowshoes have wooden frames and are beautiful pieces of craftsmanship. Their natural materials have the color, the history, and the warm, human touch that sport snowshoes sacrifice for their lightweight, high-technology components. But before you can put away a pair of traditional snowshoes at the end of winter, you'll need to waterproof the webbing and the bindings, a process that requires removing the harness and applying a resin-based spar varnish. Each year the bindings also need to be treated with a coat of high-quality wax. Only then may you store the shoes in a place that is dry, cool, and mouse free.

The advantages of sport snowshoes, made from aluminum, rubber, and other "high-tech" materials, are durability, ease of use, and low upkeep. Sport snowshoes require no maintenance and are rugged enough that many companies provide lifetime warranties. At the end of a season, you can pitch your sport snowshoes anywhere, and they'll be ready to go for the next season with no loss in their life span.

Anatomy of a Snowshoe

There are five parts to most snowshoes: the frame, binding system, pivot system, crampons or claws, and decking. When it is time for testing, rental, or purchase, put on each pair of snowshoes and compare these parts to decide which pair best suits you.

Frames

In general, there are three different sizes of snowshoe frames: short-oval, medium-wide, and long-narrow. Because of the continuous decking material in sport snowshoes, smaller shoes get more flotation than their earlier, longer counterparts. For example, a 10-inch by 36-inch (25-cm by 91-cm) traditional webbed shoe may have a 200-pound (91-kg) carrying weight rating. Easily, an 8-inch by 24-inch (20-cm by 61-cm) sport snowshoe will provide equal if not better flotation in the same snow conditions, and at half the shoe weight.

There are only two fundamental sport snowshoe frame shapes: asymmetrical and symmetrical. The symmetrical shoe design centers the foot in the middle of the shoe. The asymmetrical design is shaped in a curve similar to that of the human foot, which allows the binding to be set to the inside and the feet to be brought closer together. This design helps eliminate the characteristic "snowshoe waddle."

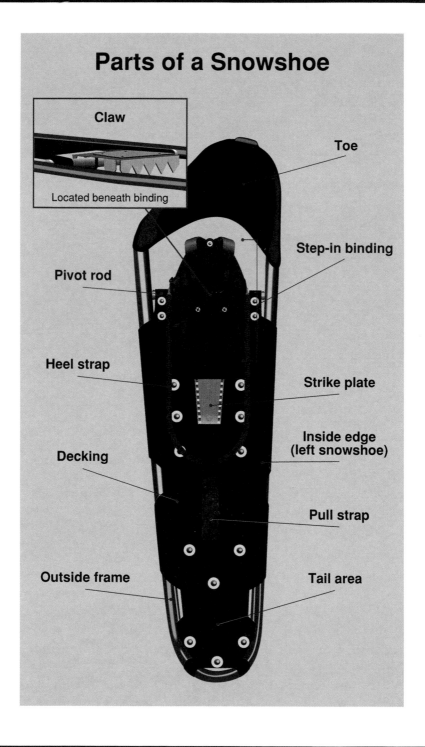

Parts of a Snowshoe

Claw

Located beneath binding

Toe

Step-in binding

Pivot rod

Heel strap

Strike plate

**Inside edge
(left snowshoe)**

Decking

Pull strap

Outside frame

Tail area

All sport snowshoes have turned-up toes in front, as this prevents snow from collapsing on the shoe and makes it easier to move forward. For the same reasons, most modern snowshoes are weighted such that the tail is heavier than the toe, which keeps the tail down during movement.

Traditional snowshoes come in two basic shapes: elongated teardrop or oval. The teardrop shoes tend to be of two types: the long, narrow (10-inch by 56-inch, or 25-cm by 142-cm) shoes with 5- to 6-inch (13-cm to 15-cm) upturned toes, called the Alaskan or Yukon; or the shorter Maine and Michigan shoes (about 12 inches by 48 inches, or 30 cm by 122 cm). Both models are good for travel in wide open spaces and deep snow. The Ojibwa is similar to the Alaskan but is made from two pieces of wood, resulting in a pointed toe that cuts through deep snow and is less likely to load up; this makes for a much faster shoe.

Oval shoes are called "bearpaws" and are wider and shorter than the teardrop styles. Standard bearpaws range from 12 inches by 24 inches (30 cm by 61 cm) to 15 inches by 33 inches (38 cm by 84 cm) and have a 1- to 2-inch (2.5-cm to 5-cm) upturned toe. More popular for recreational users are the modified bearpaw shoes called "Green Mountain bearpaws," which are 10 inches by 36 inches (25 cm by 91 cm) and have about a 4-inch (10-cm) upturn to the toe. Green Mountain bearpaw snowshoes maneuver well in thick brush and densely forested areas and are great for use around camp.

Binding Systems

Traditional snowshoes are held on your foot by rawhide harnesses called either "A" or "H" bindings, depending on their shape. Sport snowshoes have replaced the rawhide harness with bindings adapted from those used in cycling or skiing. The most advanced sport bindings work in coordination with the pivot system. Whether you are buying traditional or sport snowshoes, look for bindings that provide a solid landing platform and a secure connection between you (your shoe) and the snowshoe.

Our criteria for bindings are ease of use, little lateral or fore/aft motion, no pressure across the foot, universal fit (one size fits all), use of buckles or quick release systems (no lacing), and proper heel positioning (no contact with the frame). If you look for these qualities, you won't go wrong.

Pivot Systems

The pivot system is a high-stress point in a snowshoe and needs to withstand considerable weight and rotational forces simultaneously. Pivot systems using thick rubber straps allow for limited rotation as the foot flexes.

Sport Snowshoe Models

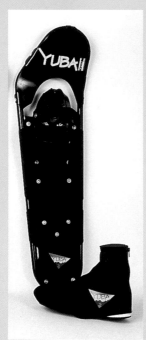

Back-Country Models

These one-size-fits-all models are the real workhorses of snowshoes. They'll get you through deep snow, but not very quickly. All are at least 8 inches wide by 30 inches long (20 cm by 76 cm), and may weigh 2 to 3 pounds (1–1.4 kg) per shoe. You can usually find a pair for about $200 to $250.*

Walking and Recreational Models

These all-purpose snowshoes combine good flotation with lighter weight and better maneuverability. Widths are generally no more than 10 inches (25 cm) and lengths should be under 32 inches (81 cm). Walking models weigh less, too—around 2 pounds (1 kg) each. The cost is also a little less—around $160 to $200 per pair.

Cross-Training Models

With cross-trainers you begin to move into the real sport models of snowshoes. The dimensions should be small (under 9 inches [23 cm] in width and 26 inches [66 cm] in length), and the weight could be as low as 1 pound (.5 kg) per shoe. You'll pay a little more for cross-trainers—about $200 to $210 a pair.

Racing Models

These are the true elites of sport snowshoes. Racing models are very small (8 inches [20 cm] or less in width, and less than 25 inches [64 cm] in length) and very light (generally 1 pound [.5 kg] or less per shoe). Racing snowshoe bindings are often sized to fit, and some allow for direct mounting of your athletic shoes to the frame. For direct mount models, expect to pay around $160 to $180; for standard-binding models, around $210 to $250 per pair.

*Prices are in U.S. dollars.

Snowshoes with this "stationary pivot system" (SPS) are ideal for hard-packed trails because they provide a rebound effect and don't allow the snowshoe to drop away from the foot as the foot pushes off from the snow. On the other hand, rotational pivot systems (RPS) allow for the tail of the snowshoe to drop away from your heel and the front of the shoe to rise, which keeps snow from building up on the toe. There is also a modified RPS, which uses a return system, thereby providing the best features of SPS and RPS.

Crampons and Claws

Sport snowshoes come equipped with either crampons or claws, depending upon their intended use. These are the parts of the snowshoe that provide traction and are particularly necessary in conditions where ice or steep terrain are common. Crampons are usually made from heat-treated aluminum or tempered carbon steel and are generally attached to the pivot rod. Most crampons have three to five "points" in the front that are a half inch to 1 inch (1.3–2.5 cm) in length. Lateral points are also common, adding much-needed traction and stability when traversing. Rear points for additional traction also help in icy con-ditions.

A claw is like a crampon but less spiky; its serrated teeth are half the length of average crampons. Claws are used on racing snowshoes or in conditions with little ice or few steep surfaces. Serrated or smooth angle claws are not adequate for the ice crust that forms above the treeline in cloudy, subfreezing weather, however.

There are drawbacks to the use of claws and crampons. It is possible (although difficult) to fall onto the crampons, which can cause injury. Also, wet snow tends to pack into crampons because of their configuration, which can be dangerous because traction is lost when balls pack between the points. Finally, if you enjoy snowsliding, a claw seriously impairs your ability to glissade down a slope.

Decking

The decking is attached to the snowshoe frame and provides the majority of the shoe's flotation. Most sport snowshoe decks are made of Hypalon, a rubberized synthetic material. Decks come in various weights and are attached with aluminum rivets. In traditional snowshoes, the decking is attached with either synthetic or rawhide lacing. Several companies also make plastic deckings, which have a slick surface and are correspondingly slick on the snow.

Most decking includes a return system, which limits the shoe's range of motion when pivoting. Without a return, the toe of the shoe can swing upward and nick your shins. Also, when you are jumping, the return system prevents the tail from landing perpendicular to the ground and thus places the shoe in the best and safest position to absorb your weight.

Deciding What to Buy

We can't emphasize enough that shoe weight and size are critical in snowshoeing. It is estimated that 1 extra pound (.5 kg) on the foot equals 5 to 10 pounds (2.3–4.5 kg) of weight on your back. Also, narrower is always better than wider, because width in the frame tends to make movement more difficult and awkward. It also slows you down to have wider shoes because your legs extend outward from the hip sockets rather than moving directly underneath you.

Think of what type of snowshoeing you'll be doing and where you will be doing it before deciding on the snowshoe model and specifications. There is no one best sport or traditional snowshoe for everyone for every day. If you are a racer or cross-trainer in an area with well-packed snow, you can look for a small sport snowshoe. If you are a walker or recreationalist, consider a slightly wider and longer snowshoe. If you are a back-country enthusiast or a winter camper, you'll probably run into a fair amount of unpacked powder; in that case, look for a large snowshoe with enhanced flotation and good traction.

When you buy, do keep in mind the key difference between sport and traditional snowshoes: Because the decking on traditional snowshoes is not continuous, their flotation is not as great, so the mass of the wearer and the conditions that prevail where you will be snowshoeing will be more important. Traditional snowshoers need to check a size/weight chart for specifics on snowshoe dimensions appropriate for their fully laden weight; most snowshoe retailers keep these size/weight charts around for you to use. On the other hand (or, in this case, the other foot), if you are using sport snowshoes, because of their solid decking and resulting high flotation, what you do with the shoes matters more than how much you weigh. Thus, sport snowshoers follow "use" charts like the following to decide which model to select.

Sport Snowshoe Use Chart

Use	Width of snowshoe*		
	Up to 8 inches (20 cm)	8 to 10 inches (20–25 cm)	10+ inches (25+ cm)
Walking/touring	×	×	
Back-country hiking or camping		×	×
Cross-training	×	×	
Racing	×		
With snowboarding	×	×	
Ice climbing	×	×	
With snowmobiling		×	×
Mountaineering		×	×

*If the snow in your area is particularly dry and powdery, consider choosing the next larger size snowshoe, as drier snow requires greater flotation.

SNOWSHOE MYTHS

When you go out to buy or rent your first snowshoes, keep in mind that there are a few long-held myths that a well-meaning outfitter might try to pass along. The truth is, snowshoes are evolving so rapidly that it is difficult for retailers to keep up with all the new features, especially for sport snowshoes. So, while it is definitely a good idea to consult the salesperson for help when you buy, keep in mind that sometimes you, the customer, might really know best.

Myth 1: If I am big, I need a big snowshoe.

Body size is not the most important factor in determining how large sport snowshoes need to be. Rather, the key factor is the amount of moisture in the snow. In very dry, powdery snow, everybody sinks—no matter how large or small they or their snowshoes are. And in moist, heavily compacted snow, a small racing snowshoe will do for even the biggest snowshoers. For a 150-pound (68-kg) person, the difference in sinkage between a 24-inch (61-cm) and a 32-inch (81-cm) sport snowshoe is only 3 inches (7.6 cm) in normally hydrated snow conditions.

Myth 2: Frame shape doesn't matter.

The fact is, frame geometry (the length, width, and shape) is one of the most important features of a snowshoe. Most snowshoes are completely symmetrical, with the foot centered over a pivot system slightly forward of the body's natural balance point. However, some newer snowshoes are built asymmetrically to match the geometry of human feet, thereby providing better balance and control and a more natural feel in use.

Myth 3: The bigger the claw, the better.

Claws come in different sizes, depending on your preference and, most important, the type of terrain you generally encounter. For lightweight racing snowshoes, lightweight claws are usually most appropriate. It is primarily the back-country snowshoer or mountaineer who requires the extra traction of a bigger claw.

Myth 4: Boots are the preferred snowshoe footwear.

While this may be true for the back-country snowshoer, for recreational sport snowshoers—walkers, runners, or cross-trainers—the shoe of choice is a walking, running, or cross-training shoe. Wearing your normal training shoe inside a neoprene snowshoe bootie allows for the best of both worlds—you get the comfort of an athletic shoe and the pleasure of warm, dry feet.

Dressing for Success

What you'll want to wear and take when shoeing depends on the snowshoeing activities you're planning to pursue and the winter conditions you'll likely face. You can probably open your closet and come up with enough suitable gear to keep you comfortable and equipped on your first couple of snowshoe outings.

It's been said before, but it doesn't make it less true: There is no such thing as bad weather. Wearing the wrong clothes and shoes at the wrong time is what makes for bad weather. Mainly, your apparel and accessory needs, like your snowshoe needs, depend on what you are doing out there in the snow:

For walking and recreation, dress for the ambient conditions. Always dress in at least two, if not three, layers so that you will have maximal protection from the cold, as well as options if it warms up.

© John Kelly

The typical outing requires little specialized gear.

For training and racing, simply dress as if you were going to cross-country ski or run in winter conditions. The "25-degree rule" applies here: Take the ambient temperature, add 25 degrees Fahrenheit (about 15 °C), and dress as if you were going to be exposed to that temperature. That's the effect of the warmth you will feel from the heat you are generating. Always bring along clothes for colder conditions, though, because weather can change rapidly and you'll need to be prepared. Also, when you stop, the 25-degree rule goes out of effect, and you will feel not only the ambient temperature but also the effects of the moisture on your skin evaporating.

Footwear

This is where it all begins: If your feet are warm and comfortable, you'll be happy; if your feet are miserable, you'll be miserable. That said, if you are just starting out, we suggest that you wear whatever footwear you already have for your initiation into snowshoeing. For example, snowmobile boots will work, but they are rather heavy and clumsy for long-term use. Cross-country ski boots will also work temporarily but don't provide much in the way of foot support.

If you decide you like snowshoeing enough to do it regularly, you will want to purchase footwear that allows you the most comfort and dexterity. The rule for footwear is the same as for the rest of your equipment and snowshoes: the lighter, the better. Heavy leather or double plastic boots are great for climbing over exposed rocks, but in areas where the rocks are covered and there is no need for ice crampons, you pay the price in encumbrance. The GI/Korea boot (also called the Mickey Mouse, mouse, or bunny boot), heavy mountaineering boots, and commercial leather insulated boots all work well for the ultimate in cold-weather protection. However, when choosing a boot, make sure that you get a pair that is not so rigid that your ankle can't flex. Also, avoid boots with hard or sharp heels because they will abrade and wear through your decking quickly.

Your first choice for sport snowshoeing can be as simple as lightweight athletic shoes or hiking boots. However, you must wear booties or a pair of gaiters over these to keep your feet warm. If you are a winter camper and on flat terrain, soft boots are probably best.

Tradition may play as much of a role as performance in your footwear decision. In cold, dry snow, the footgear for traditional snowshoers is Indian-style moccasins, adapted with felt liners and worn with extra socks. When Alaska native Benjamin Allen beat Shawn Lyons in the 1993 Iditashoe race, he wore his mukluks, a high-rising Native American moccasin, the entire distance. Maybe there is something to say for custom footwear sans midsoles, arch supports, and nylon uppers, if that's what you're used to.

Booties

As you know, it's really annoying to get your feet wet and cold. The simple solution, especially when you are wearing athletic footwear (cross-trainers, walking shoes, racing flats, etc.), is to slide into a neoprene bootie. Booties are essential if you want to cover the gap between your pants and the top of your footwear. With a center band that attaches underneath, a bootie covers your entire shoe, leaving exposed only the rear and front of the sole. Booties come in several sizes and typically have a rear-entry system and a Velcro closure along the top to prevent snow from entering.

Booties and gaiters help keep your feet warm and dry.

Gaiters

They look like spats, covering the ankle, instep, and lower leg, but they are made of water-repellent fabrics. The drawback: They leave the top of your boots or shoes exposed. If you are snowshoeing in heavy hiking boots, gaiters work great, so use them. Gaiters come in two lengths: long, which reaches just below the knee, and short, which covers about 2 inches (5 cm) above the top of the boot. Super gaiters are heavy nylon overboots that extend up to the knees. They are insulated and are a must for extremely cold temperatures, as they double the warmth of a single boot. They usually have a front zipper to provide you access to your boots or shoes.

Tops and Bottoms

High-fashion ski gear may look fantastic, but it generally doesn't work for snowshoeing. Wearing tight-fitting nylon jackets and elasticized pants may not keep you warm and dry or allow free, comfortable movement. What works best? Modern running apparel is a good bet, as is anything else that provides layerability, breathability, and movability. If you can't run in it, don't try to snowshoe in it.

Each layer you wear increases the amount of "dead air" that surrounds and insulates your body. Thus, the more layers, the more warmth. But you layer not only for warmth but for coolness as well. As you move, your body starts to heat up, and if you can't adjust your apparel to cool off, you'll begin to sweat and risk dehydration (or even hypothermia from your dampened clothes).

For your innermost (underwear) layer, wear fabrics that wick moisture away from your skin. Over that, wear a thermal layer to keep you warm. Finally, your outer layer should be both wind and water repellent. The more layers you wear, the more options you have for controlling your body's temperature.

For breathability, you want what are called "pull/push" or "hydrophilic/hydrophobic" garments made of synthetics and blends that are widely available at sporting goods stores. Within the same piece of clothing, the hydrophilic fabric "loves" perspiration and draws your sweat away from you, through the fabric, to the hydrophobic layer, which "fears" moisture and releases it to the outside. These properties are primary requisites for your first (underwear) layer. Avoid cotton—it dries slowly and once wet won't keep you warm.

So, you will need three tops, each corresponding to one of the aforementioned layers. There should be a ventilation layer next to your skin, usually made of a pull/push fabric; a middle, thermal layer of a material with loft, like polar fleece or down; and a water- and wind-proof layer on the outside.

For bottoms, follow the same guidelines as for tops, with an added emphasis on range of motion, as it is your legs that do most of the moving. Choose an outer layer pant with a leg-length zipper so it can be easily removed or adjusted to compensate for body temperature changes. In fit, your bottoms shouldn't be too baggy, but it is more vital that they not be too tight. Tight pants restrict movement and prevent insulating layers of air from forming between your skin and your clothes.

Accessories

You don't need a lot of extra accoutrements for an enjoyable snowshoeing experience, but the right accessories can help make a good thing even better.

Headgear

Considered the most representative piece of winter apparel, hats are inexpensive, colorful, and a necessity. Why? If you haven't heard already, take note now: More heat is released from your head than from any other body part. Look at any skier's or snowshoer's hat and you'll see that it is covered by the hoarfrost that forms as a result of the heat and moisture that escape from the scalp. Hats are also a good way to release heat—remove your hat and feel your body cool. The best material: hydrophilic/hydrophobic. The best color(s): bright, for safety reasons. For added warmth try earbands.

The traditional headgear for snowshoers is the knitted tuque (pronounced *took*), with its trademark tassel affixed to the top. On sunny days, try a cap with a visor to shade your eyes from the snow's reflected light. The balaclava, also known as a face mask or monk's hood, is a necessity in extreme cold.

© R. Bossi

The right clothing and accessories can increase your enjoyment.

Gloves

On most days, a lightweight glove made from a pull/push fabric (or even cotton) is all you'll need. On chillier days, remember that mittens are warmer than gloves. The warmest of all is a combination of three hand coverings: a thin inner glove to keep your fingers warm when you need them free for dexterous manipulation, an insulated glove or mitten for the middle layer, and a water- and wind-proof outer shell.

Sunglasses

Sunglasses are a must to protect you from exposure to damaging ultraviolet rays and glare. What lens color is best will depend on atmospheric conditions: Choose gray or green for bright days and amber/yellow for overcast days, as this shade will enable you to see dips in the snow. In general, avoid pink/red or blue shades.

Photochromic lenses —those that lighten in subdued light and darken in bright sun—work very well with snow. For the brightest days, choose a lens with maximum absorption (85% to 90%). Coated lenses, mirrored on the outside, are great. Select one with varied "gradient densities," which means that the top and bottom thirds of the lens will be more heavily coated than the center.

You'll find that glare can penetrate from the edge of sunglasses, so don't hesitate to get accessories to cover the sides. In windy and cold conditions, goggles work better than glasses.

SAFETY TIP *All* glasses and goggles fog. Don't live in denial—bring along a small piece of cloth with antifogger, and you'll be prepared.

The Well-Equipped Snowshoer

Although there is a long list of recommended equipment for an overnight or even a 1-day snowshoe outing (see the checklist at the end of this chapter), the following are common key pieces of snowshoeing gear.

Snowpoles

Most cross-country and trail snowshoers use poles for maneuverability and balance. Some use only one pole, as balance is much better on snowshoes than on skis. So, why use a snowpole at all? They come in very handy when you are moving forward, backward, or turning. They also provide leverage for getting up after falling, braking when downhilling, and support for crossing fences, trees, or other obstacles. Snowpoles come in many shapes and sizes, so be aware of the following variables:

- Shaft length and compactibility. To test for correct shaft length make sure your elbows are at 90-degree angles when your hands are holding the grip. Some poles can adjust in length and often come in two or three parts. The more parts, the easier the pole will be to collapse and carry in your pack when conditions permit poleless snowshoeing.

- Weight. There are many very lightweight poles made with enhanced materials out there. Keep in mind that there will be a cost of work load versus cost in dollars trade-off.

- Basket size. Select a pole with a large basket, as much as 6 inches (15 cm) in diameter. In icy or rough conditions, some snowshoers prefer a long-handled ice ax, with a basket attached to the point end as a walking aid.

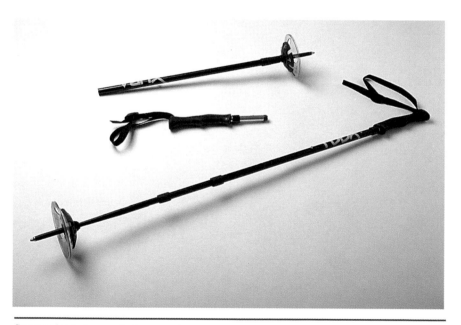

Snowpoles help you balance and maneuver.

Food and Drink

What you eat while snowshoeing can be key to your success and enjoyment, so bring along the foods that you most enjoy. Plan in advance and place your foods in freezer bags with notes telling you what they are and what meal they are for. Always take more than you think you will eat. The "more is better" rule definitely applies when you are out in the winter cold, miles from civilization.

Note, too, that proper hydration will get you extra miles. Avoid coffee, as it is a diuretic, and you'll lose as much fluid as you gain from drinking it. Instead, put some hot water in a thermal container or insulated water bottle so that you can enjoy hot chocolate or another hot drink for lunch. Sport drinks can replenish lost minerals, but try them in advance to make sure you like them. Finally, drink according to time, such as every 30 minutes, not thirst—in cold weather your sense of thirst can be dangerously distorted.

SAFETY TIP   Dehydration is very common among beginners in any sporting activity. Remember to bring along hydrating liquids, and drink!

Where to Find It All

Renting is a good way to try out a particular brand or style of snowshoes with a very low investment. Snowshoes are available as rentals from outdoor retail shops and from manufacturers (usually at sponsored events such as races).

Of course, outdoor retail shops are great for all kinds of snowshoeing-related purchases—shoes, gear, clothing, and so on—and you can usually find many stores right at or near your local snowshoeing or skiing areas.

Don't forget mail order as an option for purchasing snowshoes. Buying direct from the manufacturer can give you the added bonus of being able to voice your questions and concerns to the people who will know the most about the products. You can find a list of snowshoe manufacturers and contact information in the appendix.

Once you have your snowshoes and gear, finding clothes is the easy part. Mail order catalogs and sporting goods stores offer wide ranges of apparel suitable for the walker, runner, hiker, or camper; from Lycra to down to flannel, you can easily find what you want by asking.

EQUIPMENT CHECKLIST

Although you shouldn't consider this list of important items complete—because there are always more items to try—use it as a starting point to help you think through the clothes, gear, tools, equipment, food, and drink that you may need. Whether you're planning a 2-hour outing or a 5-day trip, you need to think ahead about all of your gear.

Clothing

Inner Layer
- [ ] Tights
- [ ] Long-sleeve shirt
- [ ] Inner socks
- [ ] Earband
- [ ] Neck gaiter/scarf
- [ ] Thin gloves
- [ ] Balaclava

Middle Layer
- [ ] Long-sleeve, polar-fleece shirt
- [ ] Polar-fleece pants
- [ ] Sweater
- [ ] Outer sock
- [ ] Down/synthetic vest or jacket
- [ ] Insulated gloves

Outer Layer
- [ ] Jacket or anorak
- [ ] Overpants
- [ ] Overgloves or overmittens
- [ ] Booties or gaiters/coveralls
- [ ] Hat
- [ ] Sunglasses

Equipment

- [ ] Snowshoes
- [ ] Snowpoles
- [ ] Ice ax
- [ ] Waterproof sunscreen
- [ ] Maps
- [ ] Compass
- [ ] Hand and pocket warmers
- [ ] Backpack or fanny pack
- [ ] Waterproof matches
- [ ] Plastic police whistle
- [ ] Flagging
  (to mark your trail)
- [ ] Cash
  (in case of emergency)
- [ ] Pencil
- [ ] Candle
- [ ] Flashlight and/or
  headlamp
- [ ] Extra batteries
- [ ] Flares
- [ ] First-aid kit

Tools	Food and Drink
☐ Leatherman with leather punch	☐ Minimum one quart (about 1 L) water (in thermal container)
☐ Duct tape (to repair snowshoes)	☐ Dry soup, oatmeal, fruit, chocolate, nuts, energy bars
☐ Rope or nylon cord	
☐ Sewing kit	
☐ Spare parts	

3

SNOW-
SHOEING
CORRECTLY

One of the finest aspects of snow-
shoeing is its simplicity. The basics of snowshoeing are without a doubt the
easiest of any activity you will ever learn, other than walking and running.
You can easily teach yourself without the need of a video or a trainer.
Anyone at almost any age with little or no sports background can snowshoe
their first day and be almost as good as the best.

Perhaps because of this simplicity snowshoeing doesn't always get the
respect it deserves. For example, last year Sally took a 3-day winter survival
course. Each of the students arrived with the required gear list, which
included a heavily loaded backpack, mountaineer skis, and boots. Sally also
took her snowshoes.

The goal was to peak California's Mount Lassen. At 10,457 feet (3,187 m), Lassen is an easy mountain in the summer but not so simple in the winter. Everyone else skied, but Sally wore her showshoes while she pulled her sled. Starting at about 4,000 feet (1,219 m), the group step-climbed and kick-stepped their way up the mountain for about 4 hours.

The next day the group stayed put halfway up the mountain and learned about winter first aid, avalanches, snow crystals, and digging snow caves. On the third day the group woke early to high winds and darkening skies, but they geared up and started the summit attempt.

Skiers had their work cut out for them, sliding heavy skis up the mountainside. In Sally's case, however, it was merely a matter of keeping her balance while lifting a 20-ounce (567-g)snowshoe with each step. And, while the mountain crampons on the snowshoes were more than sufficient for the climb, the skiers were forced to eventually drop their skis and don ice crampons.

© F-Stock/David Epperson

Snowshoes make wintertime "getting away from it all" easier.

After the exhausting climb, the group stayed at the summit only as long as it took to feel the satisfaction that they had made it—a matter of minutes.

Heading down Lassen, the skiers made long, graceful turns and Sally could enjoy the gravitation-free feeling of downhill snowshoeing. Once you have tried it, you too will know that the real thrill of snowshoeing is the downhill. Take a step and, with easy grace, you can float for several yards or meters if the conditions are right, and the powder will come up to your knees or waist and slide on by you.

Returning to the campsite, the party picked up their gear and headed down the mountain. The skiers were so fatigued by this time that they kept falling and had to take their packs off before they could even stand up again.

Finally, one man couldn't go on. Sally took his pack and put it on her sled. He took off his skis and slowly walked those last miles. He had come to appreciate the uses of snowshoes, and maybe next time he'll try a pair himself.

NO, NO, NO

If you can remember only these three admonishments, you'll be well on your way to mastering snowshoeing technique.

Never cross tails. If you step on the rear or stationary shoe with the forward-moving shoe, you will almost always fall face first in a nose-dive.

Never back up. Snowshoes don't know reverse. If you step backward, you'll drive the tail into the snow and place the snowshoe perpendicular instead of parallel to the sole of your shoe, which will generally cause a fall. Instead of backing up, take small steps to make a U-turn.

Avoid traversing. Snowshoes really aren't designed to grip with their sides. Avoid cutting across slopes, which requires digging in with the edge of the snowshoe rather than the sole or decking, if possible.

Stepping Out

When starting out, we recommend that you first snowshoe on level ground. The horizontal basics are quickly mastered, and once you have them down you can quickly "go vertical."

Striding

With symmetrical snowshoes, as your back foot swings forward, you need to adjust your stride to allow for the width of the shoe to clear, swinging each foot out and around in a semicircular arc to clear the ankle. If you don't mind accentuating the snowshoer's waddle, just keep your feet apart and you won't need to swing them around as much. If you are using asymmetrical snowshoes, you can walk naturally with no outswing and no waddle.

Stamping

Stamping produces changes in snow structure such that with each succeeding step on the same footprint, the snow hardens and a firmer base forms. When you stamp your feet, you should step lightly, pause, then place your weight. If you try both to stamp and place all of your weight on the shoe simultaneously, you will sink deeper than if you had not tried to stamp at all. As you move forward, you'll find that a very slight pause at the end of each step allows the snow to consolidate even more for the trailing shoers.

Turning

Called "kick" or "step" turns, this turning technique allows you to reverse your direction as you would if you were skiing. Plant your pole alongside

When turning with your pole next to the binding of your forward shoe, swing the back shoe around 180 degrees.

the binding of your forward snowshoe, shift your weight onto the forward snowshoe and pole and turn 180 degrees. Swing the back shoe around to point in the new direction, and stamp it into the snow. Make sure you don't cross tails or step on the back of the front snowshoe with the rear one. Plan your path in advance, choosing the easiest routes and the gentlest places on the slope to navigate your turns.

Breaking Trail

When breaking trail, keep your stride lengths short and start steps with the tail of the shoe to prevent the toe from collecting snow. Since trail breakers exert nearly 50% more energy than those following in their footprints, the lead should be rotated. Usually the trail breaker leads for 2 to 5 minutes and then steps aside to fall into the rear. Taking turns breaking trail allows the entire party to move faster over the trail.

The most difficult trail breaking can be found in relatively flat country-side, where the snow might be 6 to 10 feet (1.8–3 m) deep and, with consistently cold temperatures, soft and powdery. Breaking trail here, even with the longest and widest snowshoes, means post-holing, or sinking into the snow.

Rotate the lead frequently to give the trail breaker a chance to rest.

Bushwhacking

Bushwhacking is used to snowshoe through patches of brush. Because the brush extends above the snow, you need to stop so as to sweep the thicket under your shoe. Sometimes it requires that you use your arms and shoulders to pull yourself through the bush. Be wary of stepping among the tops of short, partially buried, evergreen trees. Powder snow will fall over them and not accumulate under the branches, leaving hollows. Hapless victims who sink into these hollows must try to get free with snow on top of them and their shoes below, trapped in tree limbs.

EARTH WATCH   Step over or around small shrubs and trees that poke through the snow. Stepping on them with your snowshoes can kill plants already weakened by winter weather.

Using Poles

Place the poles to your side, not in front, and don't use them to push off like a cross-country skier does. Instead, use your poles to give you a better

Poles can help you get back on your feet after a fall.

cardiovascular workout and to strengthen your arms as they give your legs some assistance. Telescoping or variable-length snowpoles work best. On hills, you can shorten the pole on your uphill side and lengthen the one on your downhill side.

When you fall, use your poles to help you get back on your feet. If there is so much powder that you can't get your footing, lay your pole out horizontally on top of the snow, grab it around the midpoint, and use it to push off. If this doesn't work, simply loosen your bindings and pull yourself free from the shoes.

Stepping Up

In general, it's better to go uphill on the fall line than to traverse because snowshoes don't traverse well. (The fall line is the line a ball would take as it rolls down a slope.) To avoid slipping backward, take short steps, keep your head up, and place your weight on the balls of your feet for traction. Check out the crampons that come on most sport snowshoes and make sure that they have lateral points or teeth in front of the pivot rod. If the points are behind, you won't get as much traction. There are many techniques for making ascents; learn them now and apply them when appropriate.

Rest-Stepping

Rest-stepping lets you maintain an aerobic work load while allowing your leg muscles to recover. First, plant or stamp firmly with one shoe to condense the snow. Then transfer your weight onto that leg and lock the knee in place. This puts the weight on your bones and joints and allows the working muscles to rest.

Switchbacking

In open forests with widely spaced trees, snowshoers can climb a slope by breaking a trail at 45-degree angles to the fall line. Only do short switchbacks for steep and narrow slopes and use long zigzags on wider expanses—best of all, go straight uphill. But remember that neither sport nor traditional snowshoes perform well during lateral stepping or traversing because of their lack of lateral traction.

Scrambling

This is the free-for-all ascending style common in areas where the trees are so close together that the best solution is often just to scramble over the crust by the shortest route possible. When scrambling, use a technique called "walking on your toes," in which you stamp with the front of the foot to dig in the crampon and force the lateral points into the snow.

When scrambling, keep your body low and use your arms to power up the hill.

Side-Kicking

Side-kicking isn't recommended, since snowshoes aren't designed to grip with their sides; however, sometimes it is necessary to move across a slope rather than straight up or down it. Also known as "traversing," this technique is used for making diagonal steps across the face of a slope, thereby decreasing its steepness. To maintain traction when side-kicking, the uphill leg must be planted firmly, with a stamping action, digging in the forefoot and moving the heel to the uphill edge. Try to place as much weight on the uphill edge of the snowshoe as possible, as this cuts the snow and forces the uphill edge into the slope. At the same time, you'll want to plant the crampon into the hillside. The downhill leg will stamp as well, but it is extended and won't take the stress that the uphill leg can. Keep your pole planted on the uphill side for balance. If you can't maintain a hold on the hillside, resort to kick-stepping and going straight up or down.

When side-kicking, be sure to dig the outside edge of the uphill shoe into the snow, then place your weight on your uphill shoe and pole. Finally, bring your downhill foot up and dig its inside edge and cleat into the snow while using the poles for balance.

Kick-Stepping

When you kick-step (or "toe-in"), you take the front of the shoe and kick it straight into the side of the slope about 6 to 10 inches (15–25 cm). Sometimes you must make several kicks to dig deep enough to plant the

claw and shoe so they will hold weight. If the snow is unconsolidated, the steps can be very fragile, and often the trail breaker will have less difficulty than the followers, as the steps that were cut break out. The line of steps may also become an ever-deepening trench, requiring more work for those in the back. Where there is not much base under the snow, it may be better to go without your snowshoes and do a bare boot kick-step.

To kick-step correctly, kick the toe of the shoe 6 to 10 inches (15–25 cm) into the side of the slope.

Side-Stepping

With this technique you edge the snowshoe in while facing 90 degrees to the fall line. Common for skiers, side-stepping requires stamping, planting, transferring weight to the upper shoe, and then bringing the trailing shoe up to a parallel position. Kick-stepping is preferred by most shoers over side-stepping.

If you ascend by side-stepping, face across the fall line, stamp your uphill shoe into the snow, and bring your downhill foot up to meet it.

Herringbone Stepping

Use this technique to climb moderate slopes. With each step land "toe out" so that your shoe forms an angle with the pitch of the slope. Keep your knees well bent and straddle the fall line with your shoes in a reverse snowplow position. This stance is not comfortable for long, but it will provide traction when you are starting to backslide.

When herringbone stepping, keep your knees bent and your shoes in a reverse snowplow position to give you enough traction to prevent backsliding.

Downhilling

Downhills are the ultimate test of the quality of the snowshoe binding because all of your weight is driven forward into the toe piece. If the binding is an open-toe piece and the toe strap isn't tight enough, the toe will slide under the crosspiece and you'll fall face first.

Plan your descent in advance based on the pitch and the snow cover. If you're looking for some fun, try snowsliding: Lean back and draw back on the claws, forcing the toe upward; you can almost glissade down the slope with long striding, gliding steps. Some shoers prefer riding the tails of the snowshoes down a slope. You can also ride your shoes with one foot in front and the other trailing to adjust for braking. Leaning on your poles turns them into a rudder or a brake when you need to turn slightly or slow down.

Snowsliding on a descent is ample reward for a tough ascent.

SAFETY TIP For a controlled descent, use snowpoles for balance and stability, keep your weight back on your heels, and walk down slowly.

Jumping

Jumping is what teenagers and kids like most about sport snowshoeing. Try it on powder—the landing is soft. Just make sure your shoes have a return system so that your tails land first and help break the fall. Some snowshoe jumpers—the serious ones or those without return systems on their shoes— tie their heels down to the decking to guarantee a stable landing.

SKILLS CHECKLIST

With a little practice, feedback from your friends, and a video camera (not necessary, but fun), and your muscles, you'll have the following skills down in no time!

Horizontal Moves	Vertical Moves
☐ Striding	☐ Rest-stepping
☐ Stamping	☐ Switchbacking
☐ Turning	☐ Scrambling
☐ Breaking trail	☐ Side-kicking
☐ Bushwhacking	☐ Kick-stepping
☐ Using poles	☐ Side-stepping
	☐ Herringbone stepping
	☐ Downhilling
	☐ Jumping

Getting to Know the Great Outdoors

A big part of snowshoeing correctly is being aware of your environment. From watching the weather to keeping track of where you are, it is your responsibility to yourself to be an educated, aware snowshoer.

Nothing affects snowshoers more than the surface they are shoeing on. For example, whereas skiers adore the lightest and deepest powder snow, snowshoers prefer a more compacted snow base. The beauty of snowshoes is that they really can take you anywhere on any of the winter surfaces Mother Nature offers you. As long as you are careful, be it on snow or ice, you can be out there having fun.

Snow

If you become an avid snowshoer, you will learn to love your element and want to know more about it. You can learn the dynamics of snow by studying it and the conditions that affect it. For example, compressibility is a property of snow important to snowshoers. As weight is applied to snow crystals, they restructure themselves into a tighter, firmer mass. However, snow does not compress itself proportionately to the weight you put on it—which is why a 200-pound (91-kg) adult doesn't sink twice as far into the snow as a 100-pound (45-kg) adolescent.

© F-Stock/David Wheelock

Studying the snow can help you spot conditions that are perfect for snowshoeing.

In colder temperatures, new snow will be light and powdery. Freshly fallen powder snow is impossible to cross without post-holing, no matter how large your snowshoes are. However, after 2 or 3 days the powder will become firmly packed snow that is perfect for snowshoeing.

When temperatures rise and then fall, a crust will form on the snow because warmth thaws the surface and then the cold freezes it over again. You won't sink much in crusted snow, but often it's not pleasant to walk on because it can be slippery and hard.

Where snow falls affects it as well. Snow on the shaded sides of mountains and on lee slopes (the opposite side of the windward slope) is the slowest to pack and the most likely to avalanche. Snow in deep and shaded valleys and in heavily timbered areas firms slower than exposed snow and is likely to stay powdery longer. Snow on the southern sides of mountains (in the northern hemisphere, that is) can freeze overnight into a thick crust.

Wind, too, affects snow. First, wind acts as a packing agent, condensing the snow. For example, when snow is falling in windy conditions, solid slabs of snow can form that can be very unstable. Or sometimes wind can be so strong as to blow the snow off exposed terrain and pile it even deeper in sheltered areas.

Avalanches

In an avalanche you are at the mercy of tons of rapidly moving snow—a force of nature much too powerful for people to surmount. The only effective strategy for surviving an avalanche is to avoid it. To do that, you must learn to recognize areas and conditions where avalanches are likely to occur.

The most common areas for avalanches are treeless slopes, steep lee slopes, and gullies and other exposed slopes of between 25 and 45 degrees pitch. Most avalanches occur during or immediately after a snowstorm, when a large amount of fresh, unpacked snow falls on older, packed surfaces of ice and glazed snow. That's your highest danger time. But, really, anything that disturbs unstable snow—snowshoers, skiers, even an idiot maker (those huge snow-bombs that fall out of trees with a noisy "whump")—can cause an avalanche.

Many local ski and recreation areas offer avalanche safety courses that are definitely worth your while if you can find one locally. Other helpful local resources are radio and television ski reports and avalanche information hotlines. Take the time to find out what the conditions will be like *before* you arrive at your destination.

Ice

Ice, often hidden by snow, presents two potential problem areas to the snowshoer: balance and traction. Ice is a low-friction surface that can cause annoying and sometimes dangerous falls. Ice can also be deceiving. You won't forget the experience if a patch of thin ice gives way under you and you fall into a near-frozen creek or pond.

Good, sound ice will hold huge amounts of weight, but you must make sure there are at least 2 inches (5 cm) of solid ice under you when crossing over any water. Gray areas on an otherwise white-iced surface indicate thin ice. If you are near a location where a stream flows into a pond or other waterway, beware. Ice is usually poorly frozen in such areas. River ice is more dangerous than standing water because moving water freezes irregularly. Snow bridges can also form up over moving water and camouflage a danger point. When in doubt, loosen your bindings before you cross over ice so that you can remove your snowshoes quickly if you break through. Also, carry a coil of rope in your hands to help in case of rescues. If you are part of a group moving over ice, separate yourselves by 20-foot (6-m) intervals.

SAFETY TIP

Remember a basic difference between thick and thin ice: Thick ice is solid white, whereas thin ice is gray or has grayish patches. Keep your eyes open!

DON'T GO "BAREFOOT" IN THE SNOW

I'm often surprised at how many people, when talking about their recent climbs, remark, "Well, the trail was pretty well packed, so we just carried our snowshoes. We broke through here and there, but it wasn't bad at all." The clincher for me occurred a couple years back, when I was climbing in the Adirondacks. I arrived and geared up for my hike and started for the trailhead behind three other fellows who had their snowshoes lashed to their packs. I soon caught up to those three, and one of them said in a surprised tone, "Oh, you're *wearing* your snowshoes!" I replied, "That's what they're for," and proceeded on past them. He said, "If I had ones as small as yours, I'd be wearing them, too." When I arrived at the summit, a bit tired from breaking trail, I was elated with the spectacular view, which I enjoyed for about an hour before heading back down.

Nearly a mile (about 1.5 km) below the summit, I found the tracks of the three fellows I'd passed. They had made it as far as the snowdrifts before turning back. Clearly, they had exhausted themselves by sinking waist-deep with each step.

Why is going "barefoot" a real problem? First, consider your own safety. When climbing without snowshoes, I slip backward as much as I go forward, which is very tiring. A boot's small surface area doesn't grip enough and will break up the snow and the trail's surface. Then the snow will often "mush out" on all sides of the boot, greatly decreasing much-needed stability.

Next, consider the safety of those who "follow in your footsteps." Walking on a trail full of post-holes is dangerous, whether you are wearing snowshoes or not. Holes make it difficult to maintain balance, especially when you're going downhill, and there's a constant worry about twisting an ankle. Even worse, someone could break a bone by falling into a frozen post-hole.

Walking around without snowshoes in winter, particularly at the upper elevations, could be compared to running whitewater without a life preserver. Winter is a beautiful time of year, but it can also be harsh and unforgiving. Snowshoes should be regarded as necessary equipment, just as much as a warm parka and boots.

—Carl Heilman II

4

SNOW-SHOEING FITNESS AND SAFETY

We've said it before: Anyone in any condition can put on a pair of snowshoes and go! However, this is not to say that anyone in any condition can put on a pair of snowshoes and go *anywhere*.

Physical fatigue takes the fun out of any outing and snowshoeing is no different. Fatigue can also lead to making decisions like taking an unknown shortcut rather than wisely backtracking. The bottom line is that fitness is an excellent preventive measure against emergencies and the best insurance for a good time in the wintry outdoors.

Types of Conditioning

© F-Stock/David Stoecklein

Cardiorespiratory Fitness

Anything more strenuous than short-distance snowshoeing strolls on level ground requires sufficient aerobic stamina to maintain your heart rate in aerobic and higher-than-aerobic ranges for an extended period of time. Determining your cardiorespiratory fitness and controlling your levels of exertion can be easy with a heart rate monitor; we recommend using one for all phases of training. (*Note.* If you are interested in learning more about training with heart rate monitors, refer to *The Heart Rate Monitor Book*, by Sally Edwards. For information write to Sally at 2636 Fulton Avenue, Sacramento, CA 95825, USA, or phone 916-481-7283.)

© R. Bossi

Muscle Strength

When using poles, snowshoeing requires both upper and lower body strength. Generally, though, snowshoeing most involves three lower body muscle groups: the hip flexors, the upper leg muscles (the quadriceps, which lift the snowshoe, and the hamstrings, which move the leg forward out of the snow), and the calf muscles (which you use whenever you are pushing off with your feet or lifting onto your toes, especially on the uphills).

Flexibility

Snowshoeing demands that you stretch your body in unexpected directions at unexpected times. One particular area of flexibility should be the gastrocnemius (calf) muscle, because snowshoers are often on their toes, pushing on the uphills and stretching their calves on the way down. For this reason, thorough stretching before and after snowshoeing, for solid warm-up and cool-down periods, is highly recommended.

© John Kelly

© F-Stock/Chris Huskinson

Coordination

You'll need both coordination and balance to climb uphill, glide downhill, and negotiate rocks, trees, ice, and so on. The ways snowshoers get and stay coordinated are nearly unlimited: Dancing; sports that involve whole-body coordination, such as tennis, gymnastics, or the martial arts; skiing; and, of course, snowshoeing itself are all good choices.

How Ready Is Your Body?

You may never want to do anything more strenuous than take a nice leisurely walk on the snow. That's fine! But if you get hooked on the activity and want to make snowshoeing the springboard for a fitness program, we'll show you how. There are a couple of easy ways to determine

A well-conditioned body prepares you for many snowshoeing challenges.

if you are sufficiently fit to go snowshoeing. The first is to read through this chapter's description of the four types of conditioning and how they relate to snowshoeing and to decide if you are up to snuff in each. The second is simply to go out, stretch your muscles, and try a short (maybe an hour long) snowshoeing walk on mostly level terrain. If you find yourself winded, or too weak to walk in snowshoes comfortably, it's probably best for you to do a little fitness training before heading out for anything more strenuous.

SAFETY TIP   If you are over 40, are more than 20% over your ideal weight, or have any known or suspected cardiorespiratory problems, you should consult a physician before starting any conditioning program.

Improving Your Snowshoeing Fitness

The best way to train is to follow the principles of specificity and progression. This means training the specific muscles and support systems in the specific way they are needed in the given activity and progressively adding work load. Put simply, to be a good snowshoer you need to snowshoe, and if you want to keep improving you'll need to keep increasing the amount of snowshoeing you do.

Our snowshoe training program is presented here in three phases, each with its own fitness goal. Each phase is more challenging than the previous one, the workout session longer, and the type of workout more specific.

PHASE 1: BUILDING A BALANCED FITNESS BASE   Phase 1 is designed to build a basic fitness foundation and is not specific to snowshoeing. If you follow the format of this first phase, you'll develop a fitness base to use for any exercise pursuit—snowshoeing, mountain biking, softball, or any other activity.

				Phase 1 Training Plan			
Week	Mon	Tues	Wed	Thurs	Fri	Sat or Sun
1	Weights 20 min.		Run/walk 20 min.		Aerobics 20 min.	Stretching 25 min.
2			Same as Week 1			
3	Weights 15 min. Run/walk 15 min.		Stretching 15 min. Weights 15 min.		Aerobics 30 min.	Run/walk 15 min. Stretching 15 min.
4			Same as Week 3			

PHASE 1:

PERIOD: 4 WEEKS
DURATION: 20-30 MINUTES
FREQUENCY: 4 DAYS PER WEEK

The goal of this first phase is to get your fitness level to a point where you can exercise 20 to 30 minutes a day, 4 days a week, in the four different fitness areas, for at least 4 weeks. A couple of notes about the training chart: To "run/walk" is to alternate between each within the same workout period. For example, you may walk for 3 minutes and run for 1 minute five times for a total of 20 minutes. With time, you can lengthen the running periods and shorten the walking periods. Also, for your aerobics class, step aerobics is preferred because it does a wonderful job of strengthening the muscles you use during snowshoeing.

If you choose, you can alter the individual workouts to fit your daily schedule, and you can do them either back to back or with a day of rest in between. You can also change the workouts to suit your preferences. If you would rather climb stairs than take an aerobics class, that's fine. Just make sure you exchange one aerobic workout for another; doing four strengthening workouts a week will not get you where you want to go. It is also fine to stay in Phase 1 training for more than 4 weeks if you've been unconditioned for a while and need more time to develop your base. Make sure you are comfortable with Phase 1 training before progressing to Phase 2.

PHASE 2: BUILDING A BIGGER TRAINING BASE This next, more challenging phase is designed to raise your fitness level above the threshold of conditioning you achieved in Phase 1. Note that the workouts in Phase 2 last longer and include a larger aerobic component.

			Phase 2 Training Plan			
Week	Mon	Tues	Wed	Thurs	Fri	Sat or Sun
1	Fitness class 30 min.	Run/walk 30 min.		Aerobics 30 min.	Run/walk or Snowshoe 30 min.	Stretching 15 min. Weights 15 min.
2			Same as Week 1			
3	Weights 20 min. Run/walk 20 min.	Stretching 15 min. Fitness class 25 min.		Aerobics 30 min.	Run/walk or Snowshoe 30 to 40 min.	Stretching 10 min. Weights 10 min. Machines 20 min.
4			Same as Week 3			

PHASE 2:

PERIOD: 4 WEEKS
DURATION: 30-40 MINUTES
FREQUENCY: 5 DAYS PER WEEK

"Machines" refers to any workout machines, such as steppers, rowers, stationary bikes, or treadmills, to which you have access. Machines are challenging and fun, and as you train on the different ones you will strengthen specific muscle groups.

Your fitness class can be any such class you prefer: swimming, racquetball, running, dancing, or whatever—just make sure it's aerobic.

Again, feel free to stay in Phase 2 training as long as you need. If you are simply training for overall fitness, you can stay in it indefinitely, as long as you continue to gradually increase your work load. Longer durations and more challenging workouts are the only way to keep on the path of continuous physical improvement. However, if you're ready to focus on training for snowshoeing in particular, it is time to move on to Phase 3.

PHASE 3: SPECIFICITY TRAINING Phase 3 focuses specifically on training for snowshoeing, although it still incorporates some of the earlier cross-training workouts. During this phase, we need to work the upper body muscles used for poling as well as the areas of the lower body we mentioned before: the quadriceps, hamstrings, hip flexors, and calf muscles. Specificity also means (finally!) doing the specific activity: snowshoeing. For those of us who do not live on snow, this will mean traveling to an area where you can shoe.

Phase 3 Training Plan						
Week	Mon	Tues	Wed	Thurs	Fri	Sat or Sun
1	Run/walk 40 min.		Aerobics 40 min.	Snowshoe 40 to 60 min.	Weights, Stretching, Machines 60 min.	Snowshoe 40 to 60 min.
2			Same as Week 1			
3	Endurance snowshoe 3 to 6 miles (1.9–3.7 km) with rests (~60 min.)		Aerobic snowshoe 2 to 4 miles (1.2–2.5 km) at 70% to 75% maximum heart rate	Aerobics 40 min.	Interval snowshoe 60 min.	Hill climb snowshoe 60 min.
4			Same as Week 3			

PHASE 3:

PERIOD: 4 WEEKS
DURATION: 40-60 MINUTES
FREQUENCY: 5 DAYS PER WEEK

"Endurance snowshoeing" is a cardiovascular workout in which you maintain a steady heart rate over a long duration, with rest periods as needed to keep your heart rate under aerobic levels.

When you "aerobic snowshoe," you keep your heart rate within your aerobic training zone, 70% to 75% of maximum. (To accurately determine your maximum heart rate, see your physician for a maximum heart rate test.) So, an aerobic snowshoe workout is of a slightly higher intensity but over a shorter period than an endurance snowshoe workout.

To "interval snowshoe" is to train over intervals from 2 to 10 minutes at a higher than aerobic intensity, then slow down to aerobic levels for a briefer exercise bout. It's analogous to the run/walks we've been doing all along.

An example of an interval snowshoe workout would be to run at 80% to 85% of your maximum heart rate for 3 minutes and walk for 2 minutes.

"Hillclimbs" are tough workouts, but they build strength quickly. Most people prefer doing repeat hills of about 90 seconds duration, progressing weekly by adding more and longer repetitions.

When you are doing weight training or machine training in Phase 3, spend extra time on the stations dedicated to the calf, thigh, chest, shoulder, and hip flexor muscles.

SOLO RUN

When I moved to Minnesota, it didn't take me long to discover my favorite outdoors place to play. It's an enormous park with an extensive network of trails. Because the park is relatively undeveloped, it attracts few people, especially in winter. I visited there one frigid January night, the temperature hovering at zero Fahrenheit (–18 °C). There was nothing out of the ordinary about that particular snowshoe run, except that like most snowshoe outings, it allowed me to get a lot more from my time than just another good workout. . . .

Because of the low temperatures, I make my first steps short and fast. I pump my arms vigorously to heat the layer of air trapped inside my windbreaker. The packed snow of the parking lot gives way to deep snow on the path across the rolling field to the cross-country trails and the woods in the darkness ahead.

I lower my head and climb the first hill quickly. The sun has disappeared below the horizon, and I am now 10 minutes into the run and about a mile into the woodland. The descent from the hilltop is exhilarating as I take long, slow-motion strides. I approach an intersecting trail and decide spontaneously to leave the groomed path. My new trail is narrow, and snow-laden branches hang low to form a tunnel leading to the southern fringe of the rugged, wooded section of the park.

I am comfortable on my snowshoes, even when running quickly downhill. Some people unfamiliar with the technology of the newest shoes don't appreciate how lightweight and maneuverable they are, and how fast you can run while wearing them. My snowshoes are narrow and short—perfect for traveling over packed trails like this one.

I've been running long enough to achieve a base level of strength and conditioning, and now I can comfortably explore the seemingly endless expanses of the "superhighway through the woods." I find spending an hour on a stair climber is boring, but an hour going somewhere on snowshoes is enjoyable. There are many places like this park, for those who look.

Cruising through deep drifts, my shoes pick up and throw the snow into great white puffs behind me, illuminated by the light of the moon. Ahead, crossing the trail at a perpendicular angle, is a heavily traveled path formed by the park's prolific white-tailed deer population. The lakes here are nameless and numerous and are linked by these deer runs. I forge ahead, thinking that it's times like this that I appreciate winter as the best season for bushwhacking. The trail I am running tonight is impassable in the summer months.

Turning on my headlamp to read my watch, I am stirred from my reverie, and I realize it is later than I thought. I head for the road. Upon reaching the roadside, I am greeted by a car speeding by with its wake of swirling snow and exhaust. Spoiled by miles of running on a snow-soft trail, I regretfully remove my snowshoes for the 2-mile (3.2-km) run back to the car.

—Herb Lindsey

Snowshoeing Safely

Snowshoeing is not particularly dangerous as far as injuries are concerned. There are three keys, though, to reducing any possibility of injury. The first is to be physically ready to snowshoe. This means being stretched and warmed-up before starting, as well as being fit enough to go out in the snow and hike or run around. The second key is to be aware of your environment. Wandering around in avalanche areas or over thin ice is inviting major trouble. The third key is to set reasonable goals for any given outing. Don't go for a long hike at 10,000 foot (3,050 m) elevation unless you're sure you're ready for such an endurance test.

SAFETY TIP The most common cause of sports injuries is inadequate stretching and warm-up before participation. The 10 or 15 minutes it takes to warm up can save you a world of time in rehabilitation.

Because of the risks involved in not being in top form when outdoors in the winter, snowshoeing with preexisting injuries is not recommended unless special care is taken. For example, if you have a back injury, snowshoeing safely means going out with one or more companions on a short trek in above-freezing weather.

Beating the Elements

Although winter is beautiful, it can be dangerous. The forces of nature can present some challenges. Knowing what to expect and preparing for the unexpected will help you snowshoe safely.

Frostbite

Frostbite is painless. The only way to know that a portion of your body is frozen is to look at your skin—if it is chalky white, you have frostbite. The treatment is to thaw the frozen part by restoring circulation to the area. Mild frostbite (or "frost nip") can be controlled by holding the affected area against a warm body part—thawing must be gentle, with no rubbing or abrasion. Freezing an entire hand or foot is very serious; the affected area must be completely immobilized, submerged in warm water (105 °F, or about 40 °C), bandaged, and elevated. A frostbite victim must not walk on a frozen foot and must be evacuated to safety. The prevention for frostbite is simple: Avoid exposing your skin or wearing wet clothing, and dress for the conditions, including the effects of wind chill.

Hypothermia

During hypothermia, body temperature drops because of exposure to cold. Most cases of hypothermia occur in relatively moderate air temperatures of between 30 and 50 degrees Fahrenheit (–1 to 10 °C), but the wind compounds the chill and causes people to dangerously miscalculate and suffer undue harm.

The first symptoms of hypothermia are chills and tiredness, followed by disorientation and lack of coordination. Treatment needs to be immediate—if your clothes are wet, take them off and put on dry ones. Warm up with increased exercise. Drink fluids, especially warm ones if available. Start a camp stove or build a fire. And don't hesitate to turn back immediately if someone is cold and you can't get them warmed.

Altitude Sickness

Also called elevation sickness, this condition is caused by insufficient oxygen in the bloodstream. The first symptoms are fatigue and hard, heavy breathing. The immediate response should be to slow down or stop moving entirely so the available oxygen can get to vital organs. After resting, return to a lower elevation. It takes time for acclimatization to high altitudes and their lower levels of oxygen.

© Carl Heilman II

Rest frequently when snowshoeing in high altitudes.

Dehydration and Heat Exhaustion

It doesn't make much sense to most people that they have to worry about dehydration and heat exhaustion when they are out in the cold surrounded by miles of frozen water! However, if you are keeping up a good pace of movement, you can find yourself both overheating and dehydrating. The symptoms are a rapid pulse, nausea, and a headache. You can avoid them by drinking frequently and dressing in layers so that you can remove clothing as you heat up. The test of adequate hydration is the need to urinate once every 3 hours.

SAFETY TIP
Nowhere in the world is it recommended that you drink water out of local rivers and streams. Melting snow is generally safe as long as you dig down to a clean, untrodden layer. The best choice, though, is to bring your own water with you.

Sunburn

The cost for lack of sun protection is high enough that overcompensation should be the rule. Clothing is far and away the best blocker of sun rays, so cover yourself, especially your head; there are a variety of face and head coverings widely available for just this purpose. The second line of defense is to apply sunblock or sunscreen to any skin that remains exposed. Remember too that sunlight reflecting off the snow can burn places you forget about, including your ears, the inside of your nose, the underside of your chin, and the areas around your eyes and lips.

SAFETY TIP
Protect yourself from both sunburn and frostbite by staying covered up. There is protective gear available for every part of your exposed skin—use it!

Snow Blindness

Snow blindness is a usually temporary loss of vision accompanied by pain, tears, and swelling caused by ultraviolet light reflecting from the snow. Polaroid-type sunglasses that block the ultraviolet and infrared spectrum are a must out on the snowfields. Don't even think about going out without them.

Staying Found

It's easy to get lost outdoors in the winter, but a few basic tips will help most shoers avoid this predicament.

- **Follow a trail.** If possible, select a route with a trail and stay on it.
- **Avoid dangers.** Pick a course that avoids obstacles such as ice, crevasses, partially frozen water, and areas that look prone to avalanches. The more often you are forced to detour from your course because of obstacles, the more likely you are to get lost.
- **Use prominent landmarks.** Don't just check out the landscape once in the morning. Continue to pay attention to landmarks throughout the day.
- **Know the area.** Take time to learn about the area that you are shoeing. Look at maps and talk to locals.
- **Mark your trail.** Use flagging or wands to mark your trail in case it storms and landmarks aren't visible.
- **Write it down/tell someone.** Before departing, leave a detailed itinerary with a friend, including your destination, route, and the time frame for your trip.
- **Take a companion.** In areas that you don't know well or may not be safe, always snowshoe with a buddy or, better still, several buddies.
- **Take tools.** Always carry navigation and snowshoe repair gear: maps, a compass, duct tape, cord, and a knife are bare minimums. Know how to use them.
- **Have a backup plan.** Consider and prepare for the unexpected, from encountering a storm to being forced to spend an overnight. No one has ever regretted being overprepared.

Always take a friend when venturing to unfamiliar areas.

5

THE BEST PLACES TO SNOWSHOE

There are those lucky snow-shoers who can pick up their snowshoes and head right out into their backyard for miles of fun and adventure. But for most of us going snowshoeing requires some advance planning. Even if you are not blessed with the backyard option, there are still many ways you can take to the winter snowfields. All you really need is a pair of snowshoes, some snow cover, and a sense of adventure.

Finding the Best Local Trails

Favorite destinations for many snowshoers are the very same trails they enjoy hiking in the summer and fall. We all have favorite trails that we love to hike for the flora, the terrain, the views, the quiet. Exploring these same paths changed dramatically by a blanket of snow can be a real challenge. As much as you might know a trail like the palm of your hand in the summer, you'll find an entirely different trail in the winter. Because of this unfamiliarity you'll need to be more careful than you would in the summer when you venture out on these trails.

SAFETY TIP   When snowshoeing familiar summer trails, make sure you are equipped for a longer hike than your summertime journeys—an unexpected wrong turn without adequate water or food can turn a pleasant winter outing into a miserable one.

Some snowshoers looking for a more solitary experience head for open public lands or unpaved roads, such as the fire roads prevalent in much of the western United States. One avid snowshoer in Nevada gets his daily workout by heading up a fire road near his house every morning. He often takes a training buddy and *always* takes his dog. The advantage of snowshoeing on an unpaved road is that the terrain under the snow holds few surprises, such as rocks, small brush, or holes, that can cause injury or a broken snowshoe. Often sno-parks (parking lots in snow-covered areas) will be located near these public lands or unpaved roads. The crowds of snow enthusiasts who frequent these sno-parks rarely venture more than a quarter mile from the paved road, but that needn't be the case for you.

Park systems offer a wide variety of trails and unusually beautiful scenery. If you haven't explored them in the winter, when the crowds are gone and the snow has arrived, you don't know what you're missing. Park rangers are wonderful resources for the best routes and information about safety, animal life, and weather conditions. If possible, stop at the local ranger's office, introduce yourself to the person on duty, and discuss your proposed snowshoe route and the weather conditions.

Familiar summer trails take on a whole new look during winter months.

EARTH WATCH

Going off trail in national or other public parks contributes to the erosion and degradation of what are often very fragile ecosystems. Don't do it.

Trails to snowshoe can also be found via local hiking guides, topographical maps, or trail maps. Read up on your local vicinity or on a more distant area you would like to visit this way. Outdoor shops routinely carry a wide selection of guides.

Snowshoeing Ski Resorts and Golf Courses

While the romance of snowshoeing is often associated with venturing into the untrodden wilds, there are many beautifully cultivated trails that you will not want to dismiss merely because of their popularity. Dozens of cross-country ski resorts now offer snowshoe rentals and snowshoe passes. The advantages of snowshoeing at these Nordic resorts are the kilometers of groomed trails, well-planned trail systems, and, often, warming huts. Such areas are a safe way for beginners to become comfortable with snowshoeing. The disadvantages are the cost and the reduced sense of adventure. However, many find the trade-offs worth it.

If you're interested in snowshoeing at a local cross-country resort, be sure to call first to find out whether they allow snowshoeing and what their rules are. Some resorts are so supportive of snowshoers that they now blaze specific snowshoe trails. These trails usually consist of a cross-country track laid down by snowmobile, producing enough of a trail to follow but not so much pack that it isn't a challenge. At those resorts without specific trails for snowshoers, the rule is to stay out of the diagonal tracks laid down for cross-country skiers. If you are not sure what sort of trails you're looking at, you should ask first to make sure you don't destroy the resort's hard trail work. Not taking care creates bad blood between snowshoers and skiers and makes it harder for the snowshoers who follow you.

An option that is increasingly popular is snowshoeing at Alpine resorts. This tends to be an uphill affair, with snowshoers looking for that aerobic burn heading straight up the mountain, ignoring the chairlifts. If you like going vertical without going into oxygen debt, at most resorts you can purchase a ticket to the top of the lift for a reduced price. This will allow you access to upper trails without using all of your energy just getting there. Once there, you have the best of both worlds—wonderful views, ridge lines to follow, and snowsliding to the bottom. As with the Nordic resorts, be sure to call first to make sure snowshoeing is allowed. Most Alpine resorts that allow snowshoeing require that snowshoers stay to the side of the runs, out of the way of the skiers and snowboarders.

Finally, at least in the eastern United States, snowshoeing on golf courses has become fairly popular. Generally, golf courses offer a flat or moderately rolling terrain, sufficient to get in a good workout or nice walk. You will need to check with the course management before venturing out onto the course and, once there, try to stay clear of the sand traps and off the greens, if you can tell where they are.

Trail Etiquette

When shoeing unmaintained areas, be sure to consider trail etiquette. Venturing off a trail means disturbing the local ecology. It is easy for a heavy layer of snow to cover anything from manzanita bushes to small pines. Tromping over the vegetation on snowshoes can damage the environment and destroy the habitat of small animals. Keep in mind that erosion causes serious problems in many public lands each year; checking your map before treading is one way to be sure you are not part of the problem.

Other key points of trail manners include the obvious ones: don't litter, pack out what you pack in, and don't trespass on private property. If you don't know if an area is public or private land, find out or stay out.

United States Getaways

Because most of the United States receives snowfall for at least a portion of the winter, and for some areas well into the fall and spring, there are snowshoe areas readily accessible from most American locales. Visitors to the United States will find that combining snowshoeing with sightseeing is easy, as many of the American national parks, favorite destinations for tourists from at home and abroad, receive ample amounts of snow all winter long.

THE WEST
The western United States features an extremely wide variety of snow conditions, suitable for all tastes and abilities. With conditions ranging from the powder of the Rocky Mountains to the comparatively wet snow of the Cascades, a little bit of traveling will enable you to pursue your snowshoeing habit for nearly half the year. And this is not even counting the ice and snowfields of Alaska, which are snowshoeable nearly year-round.

We think the winter is the best time to visit Arizona's **Grand Canyon**. The snow adds to the beauty of the landscape, and the oppressive crowds of the warmer months have disappeared. There is almost never snow in the canyon itself, however, and you should call first to make sure there is ample snow on the rim. You'll also want to bring your own snowshoes, as the local Nordic center currently doesn't rent them. For road conditions and weather information, phone 602-638-7888.

The trails of **Yosemite National Park** in California have been traveled by Native Americans, frontierspeople, shepherds, the cavalry, backpackers,

Continental

1 Grand Canyon, AZ
2 Yosemite, CA
3 Eagle Mountain, CA
4 Mammoth, CA
5 Lake Eldora, CO
6 Aspen, CO
7 Summit County, CO
8 Mount Bachelor, OR
9 Mount Hood, OR
10 Park City, UT
11 Snoqualmie Pass, WA

12 Yellowstone, WY
13 Lutsen Mountain, MN
14 Mequon, WI
15 Powder Ridge, CT
16 Sunday River, ME
17 Delaware Water Gap National
　　Recreation Area, NJ
18 Adirondack State Park, NY
19 French Creek State Park, PA
20 Blue Ridge Parkway, NC
21 Monongahela National Forest, WV

and generations of hikers. Yosemite's winter grandeur is one of nature's greatest masterpieces. Snowshoeing on Yosemite Valley's floor, with its relatively low 4,000-foot (1,219-m) elevation, is usually limited to January and early February. But 15 minutes away, just off Glacier Point Road, is the popular Badger Pass area, where you are likely to find snow for several more months of the year; snowshoe rentals are available there. The Park Service marks all 90 miles (145 km) of Yosemite's trails and distributes numerous maps. Two-hour, ranger-led snowshoe hikes through the high country of Badger Pass are available with free, round-trip shuttle bus service from Yosemite Valley. Winter camping and lodge facilities are available. Write: Yosemite National Park, P.O. Box 577, Yosemite, CA 95389; or phone 209-372-0265.

Eagle Mountain is a favorite for Northern California snowshoers because the proprietor is an avid snowshoer and provides trail passes for $8* and hosts snowshoe events such as the YubaShoe Marathon and the 5K and 10K Eagle Mountain Snowshoe Series. Eagle Mountain is also a first-time

© Teri Henderson

Northern California's Eagle Mountain features several exciting snowshoe races every year.

snowshoer's delight because it offers the choice of a flat, 3-mile (4.8-km) loop as well as a hike up to the ridge line at 6,442 feet (1,964 m). Eagle Mountain is located off the Yuba Gap exit, 75 miles (121 km) north on US 80 from Sacramento. There are two warming huts and plans for a hut-to-hut overnight snowshoeing system. Write: Eagle Mountain Cross-Country Ski Area, 15250 Ventura Blvd. #710, Sherman Oaks, CA 91403; or phone 800-391-2254.

Mammoth is one of Southern California's most popular winter attractions. You might want to choose a trail pass from Mammoth Cal-Nordic, the cross-country ski area that offers instruction, rentals, and tours as well as mountaineering amenities. It's a 6-hour drive from Los Angeles and boasts an average annual snowfall of 300 inches (762 cm). Write: Mammoth Ski Touring Center, Tamarack Lodge, Box 69, Mammoth Lakes, CA 93546; or phone 619-934-2442.

In the **Lake Eldora**, Colorado, area, you can travel on snowshoes with 14,000-foot (4,267-m) summits towering overhead. Stop in Boulder on your way and pick up the United States Geological Survey (USGS) trail maps so you can look over your trail options. Lake Eldora is only a 30-minute drive from Boulder and an hour from Denver. You also might want to check with David Felkley in nearby Nederland. He operates Big Foot Snowshoe Tours and leads about 20 snowshoe tours each winter. Write: David Felkley, Big Foot Snowshoe Tours, P.O. Box 1010, Nederland, CO 80466; or phone 303-258-3157.

Famed for many reasons, **Aspen**, Colorado, provides snowshoers with ample challenges and a warm welcome. An informal snowshoe group meets at the base of the Aspen lifts every morning at 8:00 and works out for the half hour to hour it takes to assault the uphill from directly under the lift poles to the top. You can also take a shuttle bus from the Hotel Jerome to the ghost town of Ashcroft, which offers 24 miles (39 km) of lonely cross-country trails for a small trail fee. Write: Ashcroft Ski Touring, Box 1572, Aspen, CO 81612; or phone 303-925-1971.

Summit County is the home of some of Colorado's best snowshoeing areas: Vail, Dillon, Keystone, and Breckenridge. Be prepared for the high altitude—almost all of the terrain is 10,000 feet (3,048 m) and above. This is where the Colorado powder is its lightest, and if you are off groomed trails, you might appreciate bringing along a back-country–size pair of snowshoes. Try the Arapaho Forest near Keystone for its numerous trails in the Montezuma Valley. There's no fee, and the trails are marked and maintained and offer exploration of long-deserted mining towns. Write: Keystone Resorts, Box 38, Keystone, CO 80435; or phone 303-468-2316.

Bordering the Three Sisters Wilderness Area and only a 20-minute drive from the city of Bend, Oregon, **Mount Bachelor** is great for day snowshoeing because of the number of forest service trails available. If you are inclined

*All prices in chapter 5 are in U.S. dollars.

to gentler environs, the Mount Bachelor Nordic Resort offers everything you could possibly desire, including a snowshoer's trail pass and frequent snowshoe races. You may want to call in advance for a list of snowshoe and ski activities. Write: Mt. Bachelor Cross-Country Center, P.O. Box 1031, Bend, OR 97709; or phone 503-382-2442 (ask for the Cross-Country Center).

Providing an entire region of high-altitude terrain and snowshoe opportunities 12 months a year, **Mount Hood**, Oregon, is one of the few places in the continental United States where you can snowshoe in August, as the resort runs their ski lifts even then to the top of the bowl. Those seeking quieter surroundings can find forest service roads in abundance—and they don't snowplow or snowmobile them during the winter. Stop at the ranger station on the drive up, where you can get maps and check on specific trails. One of our favorite trails starts at Still Creek Road and Highway 26 and continues for 4.5 miles (7.2 km) across open land, with a circle of Trilium Lake. Write: Mount Hood National Forest, 2955 NW Division St., Gresham, OR 97030; or phone 503-666-0771.

In **Park City**, Utah, you can find old mining trails and routes that take you from mining claim to mining claim on fairly flat terrain. Park City is Utah's

© David Whitten

Spectacular scenery abounds in Park City, Utah.

biggest Alpine resort, but its older sibling, Park City West, is also fun, taking you back a century in time with its clapboard buildings and wooden sidewalks. Guides are available to hire. Contact either Norwegian School of Nature, P.O. Box 4036, Park City, UT 84060 (800-649-5322), or White Pine Touring, P.O. Box 680068, Park City, UT 84068 (801-649-8710).

In **Snoqualmie Pass**, Washington, beginners and day-trippers can take advantage of weekend nature walks, starting at the Snoqualmie Pass Visitor Information Center adjacent to the Snoqualmie Summit Ski Lodge, which are usually lead by a Mount Baker-Snoqualmie National Forest naturalist. The charge is $3 and includes snowshoes. Phone 206-434-6111 to speak to the Visitors' Center.

Awesome in the summertime, many feel that **Yellowstone National Park** in Wyoming is even more beautiful with its winter blanket of snow. The best months for this Rocky Mountain gem are December to mid-March. Beware of the snowmobiles and don't miss the main attraction, Old Faithful; when snowshoeing from the Snow Lodge, you can view the geyser at its most spectacular. Write: TWR Services, P.O. Box 528, Yellowstone National Park, WY 82190; or phone 307-344-7311.

THE MIDWEST

The Midwest or central United States is characterized by high snowfalls and water content. Although we'll mention only a couple of midwestern sites, if you live in the central United States, for 3 to 5 months of the year snow is often as close as your backyard!

Ideally situated on the north shore of Minnesota's Lake Superior, **Lutsen Resort** is the biggest of the Midwest downhill resorts, encompassing four mountains and 1,500 acres (607 ha). With its proximity to Lake Superior, Lutsen has a peculiar microclimate, featuring twice the snowfall of its neighboring areas. It's an easy 90-mile (145 km) drive northeast from Duluth or a 240-mile (386-km) drive north from Minneapolis-St. Paul. You can spend weeks traveling over the 200K North Shore Trail System, which is connected to the 35K Lutsen Trail System for the cross-country ski set. Better still, buy a chairlift ticket to the summits and enjoy the glissade downhill. Write: Lutsen Resort, P.O. Box 9, Lutsen, MN 55612; or phone 218-663-7212.

Mequon, Wisconsin, has a wonderful city park that attracts the less aggressive snowshoer. John Browning, owner of a local outdoor retail shop, recommends venturing out after or during a snowfall to discover the tracks of other creatures and enjoy the peaceful vistas. The area also hosts a Tubb's 10K Series snowshoe race, one in their national series of over a dozen such events. Write: John Browning, Wilderness Connection, 6077 W. Mequon Rd, Mequon, WI 53092; or phone 414-242-4332.

THE EAST

The Adirondacks and other public lands throughout the East are readily accessible to most of the Northeast and Mid-Atlantic states. Here the combination of thick deciduous forests, clear back-country air, and abundant fresh snowfall throughout the season can be just the salve for the urban soul.

Although it contains only 5 miles (8 km) of its own trails, **Powder Ridge** lies adjacent to some of Connecticut's most popular hiking trails. These additional 30 miles (48 km) of untracked trails are shared by skiers and snowshoers together. It's easy to find—just take Exit 17 on Route 91, and you are there. Write: Powder Ridge Ski Area, 99 Powder Hill Rd., Middlefield, CT 06455; or phone 203-349-3454.

Sunday River Ski Touring Center is one of Maine's (and all of New England's) best snowshoeing destinations. Sunday River is large and seems to offer everything, including both marked and unmarked trails. Accommodations are for the budget-minded, and you can also bring a sleeping bag and share a dorm. Part of the charm of this family-oriented center is the Covered Bridge Trail, which includes a tour through the historic bridge. Write: Sunday River Ski Touring Center, Sunday River Inn, RSD2, Box 1688, Bethel, ME 04217; or phone 207-824-2410.

Delaware Water Gap National Recreation Area is a long and narrow valley that divides the Kittatinny Range in New Jersey from the Poconos in Pennsylvania. The Pocono Environmental Education Center, 7 miles (11 km) north of Bushkill, Pennsylvania, is open to all and has a nature trail for the blind. We recommend snowshoeing where the Appalachian Trail crosses the river at Water Gap; you can head out in either direction, and it's definitely worth it to reach the top of the vistas. Be warned: At the Gap's low elevations, the season is short, running only from January 1 to March 1. Write: Delaware Water Gap National Recreation Area, Bushkill, PA 18324; or phone 717-588-6637.

The enormity of New York's **Adirondack State Park** is irresistible—with 6 million acres (2,428,200 ha), Adirondack is the largest state park in the continental United States. And, with few roads through the park, accessibility is perfect for snowshoeing, as back-country travel can be accomplished only on foot or in a canoe. We can't list here all your choices for great snowshoe outings in this area, but a few of our favorites are the Paul Smith College trail near the intersection of SR 192 and SR 30; Prospect Mountain near Lake George Village; and the Adirondack Park Visitor's Interpretive Center in Newcomb, which hosts snowshoeing activities throughout the winter. Write: Department of Environmental Conservation, 50 Wolf Rd, Room 412, Albany, NY 12233-4255; or phone 518-457-7433.

French Creek State Park sits just southeast of Reading and is one of the

© Carl Heilman II

The approach to the summit of Whiteface in the Adirondacks.

most popular parks in Pennsylvania. The park's nature center and interpretive program provide you with local information on the wild deer, turkeys, raccoons, Canadian geese, and herons that reside here or migrate through the area. There are two lakes to tour, as well as northern and southern hardwood trees within the forest to enhance the beautiful surroundings. The trails are marked, with challenges for most skill levels, but if you can, venture off-trail and enjoy the habitat of the local wildlife. Write: French Creek State Park, 843 Park Rd., Elverson, PA 19520-9523; or phone 215-582-1514.

The **Blue Ridge Parkway** encompasses three large national forests within its 38,637 acres (15,636 ha) and a spectacular 469-mile (755-km) scenic highway to delight you throughout your visit. Enjoy the interpretive programs on the human history of the region and explore the nature trails that traverse the park. Write: Blue Ridge Parkway, 200 BB&T Building, Asheville, NC 28801; or phone 704-298-0398.

A third of the United States' population lives within 250 miles (402 km) of **Monongahela National Forest**, one of the East's most scenic and wild areas, ranging over both the Appalachian and the Allegheny Mountains. Upon arrival you are treated to cascades, falls, streams, deep pools, ponds, highland bogs, forests, ledges, canyons, bold rock outcroppings, and the headwaters of three major river systems. There are 676 miles (1,088 km) of hiking and backpacking trails. Write: Monongahela National Forest, USDA Building, 200 Sycamore Street, Elkins, WV 26241; or phone 304-636-1800.

SUBARCTIC SHOEING

Held each February starting in Big Lake, Alaska (an hour north of Anchorage), the Iditashoe snowshoe race starts at a local lodge and extends north for 100 miles (161 km), with no towns, homes, or cars to be seen. There is nothing, in fact, but snowmobile trails, skijorers (cross-country skiers pulled by dogs), dog-mushing teams in practice for the upcoming Iditarod, and lots of moose.

In 1993, the race began calmly enough at 10 in the morning. The Iditashoe course is a relatively flat combination of frozen swamps covered with snow (and the winter meadows that they create), combined with forests of small trees that separate them.

At about 6:00 P.M. it turned full dark, and with no moon, my headlamp reflected off the snow crystals in a continuous shimmer of dancing reflections. It was dark for the next 16 hours.

Around 3:00 A.M., at Rabbit's Lake, I abandoned my snowshoe shuffle for an athletic walk. At that point, I thought I could finish easily in about 7 hours, but I didn't know what was ahead. As the night progressed and the hours of darkness wore on, many of us started to see things that simply were not there. For me, it was usually a log house or a building that would have been the finish line—but which turned out to be only an illusion. These hallucinations lengthened the night hours considerably.

Finally, a safety marshall rode by just after daylight and told me

> politely that I looked terrible and that I had 5 miles (8 km) to the finish. As I approached the finish, I knew I had made record time. However, there was no finish banner or clock there at the end, merely food and the warmth of friends. And that was enough.
>
> —Sally Edwards

Canadian Trails

If you are a snowshoer here, you are in luck—Canada is even snowier than the United States. Snow conditions vary from west coast to east and from the southern, well-populated border to the open wilds of the far north, so there is a trail or mountain for everyone.

BRITISH COLUMBIA
Located in central B.C., just off the famed Alaska Highway and just north of 100 Mile House, you will find the 26,000 acres (10,522 ha) of **"108"** **Recreation Ranch** to explore. There are dozens of kilometers of cross-country ski trails combining flat meadowland, rolling hills, frozen lakes, and evergreen forests with no avalanche hazard. Warming cabins and historic buildings are scattered throughout the area and other activities such as skating, tobogganing, curling, night skiing, and downhill skiing facilities are available in 100 Mile House. Write: "108" Mile Ranch, R.R. 1, 100 Mile House, British Columbia, V0K 2E0, Canada.

ALBERTA
Snow sports in western Alberta are well established—there are many lodges and endless kilometers of abandoned logging roads, seismic line cuts, muskegs (bogs), and meadows in the foothills to explore. The season is long—6 months, from end of November through May—and snow accumulations are significant—from 635 to 1,016 centimeters (250–400 in.). Alberta's star attractions are **Banff** and **Lake Louise**, 80 miles (129 km) northwest of Calgary. Around these two resort towns you'll find more than 80 kilometers (50 miles) of marked trails, with 16 routes to choose from. Write: Warden, Banff East Gate, Banff, Alberta, T0L 0C0, Canada; or phone 403-762-3600.

SASKATCHEWAN
Located in central Saskatchewan, 37 kilometers (23 miles) south from Saskatoon on Hwy 11, the **Blackstrap Provincial Park** has a 5-kilometer

YUKON
TERRITORIES

VICTORIA
ISLAND

QUEEN
CHARLOTTE
ISLANDS

NORTHWEST
TERRITORIES

BRITISH
COLUMBIA   ①
"108"
Recreation Ranch   ②
Banff & Lake Louise
• Calgary

ALBERTA

MANITOBA

SASKATCHEWAN   ③

Blackstrap
Provincial Park

• Vancouver

VANCOUVER ISLAND

Winnipeg .

1   "108" Recreation Ranch, BC
2   Banff & Lake Louise, AB
3   Blackstrap Provincial Park, SK
4   Toronto, ON
5   St. Jean, PQ
6   Québec, PQ
7   Montreal, PQ
8   The Laurentians, PQ
9   Fundy National Park, NB
10   Mactaquac Provincial Park, NB
11   Kouchibouguac National Park, NB

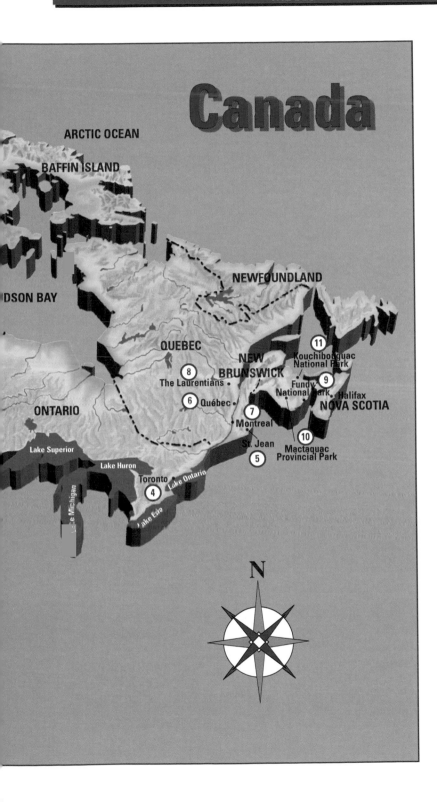

© Bill Marsh

Alberta's Lake Louise with Mount Rundle in the distance.

(3-mile) trail that is challenging but not overly difficult and graced by deciduous shrubs and trees. The area sponsors several ski races and has a day lodge, food, toboggan slide, and small ice rink with lights for night skating. Write: Travel Information, Department of Tourism and Renewable Resources, Box 7105, Regina, Saskatchewan, S4P 3N2, Canada.

ONTARIO
Toronto's parks, including High Park, the Toronto Islands, Tommy Thompson Park, and the lakefront, provide many good snowshoeing opportunities, but the most novel place to snowshoe may be the Metro Toronto Zoo. Here you can take the family shoeing or cross-country skiing past creatures great and small for a small fee.

QUÉBEC
St. Jean is the perennial site of the "Classique de Nord Américain de la Racquette" event. Hosted by Jim Tucker of Paul Smith's College, it includes snowshoe running and walking events and distances from 15K (9.3 miles) to 100 meters (328 ft). Records are kept and available if you are interested in challenging them. Write: Gaston LaBerge, 352 Franche C.P. 71, St. Luc, Québec, J2W 2A3, Canada; or phone 514-348-5455.

The city of **Québec** itself offers snowshoers 10 trail networks, including 200 kilometers (124 miles) of crisscrossed paths and city park trails. One of the best times to enjoy a visit is during Winter Carnival, a 10-day period during Lent that is billed as the "World's Biggest Winter Celebration." The other advantage to the city is that two major cross-country ski areas (**Lac-Beaufort** and **Parc du Mont Sainte-Anne**) are only a half-hour drive from downtown.

Not only is the city of **Montreal** a good snowshoeing choice with its numerous park trails, but once there you are also less than an hour's drive from the **Laurentians**. This mountain range is one of North America's top downhill and cross-country ski areas, with about 1,000 kilometers (625 miles) of trails to explore and the full range of services found only at such world-class resort destinations.

NEW BRUNSWICK

There are groomed and ungroomed public and private trails throughout this scenic province. You are almost sure to find good snow conditions from December through April, so heading out to explore on your own couldn't be simpler. Dependable choices include **Fundy National Park** (in Alma), **Mactaquac Provincial Park** (near Fredericton), and **Kouchibouguac National Park**.

Snowshoeing in the United Kingdom

Most residents of the United Kingdom will tell you to go to Scotland if you're looking for snow. The Scots are developing their ski industry to take advantage of their dependable yearly snowfall (from as early as November to as late as April or May), but the winter sport mindset is not yet pervasive anywhere in the United Kingdom. There are a few ski resort areas of note, however, and many interesting subarctic plants and types of wildlife to observe on your outings.

Scotland's foremost ski resort is in the Cairngorms, at **Aviemore**. The entire Cairngorm district, especially **Glenmore Forest Park**, offers a wide choice of winter walks. In the Grampian mountains, **Lecht** (central Scotland, near Aviemore), **Glenshee** (to the east, near Braemar), and **Glencoe** (west, near Ben Nevis, the United Kingdom's highest mountain) are also highly regarded. For more information, write the Scottish Tourist Board for their brochure "Ski Scotland": 23 Ravelston Terrace, Edinburgh, Scotland EH4 3EU.

In England, the **Pennines** range in the far north and **Lake District**

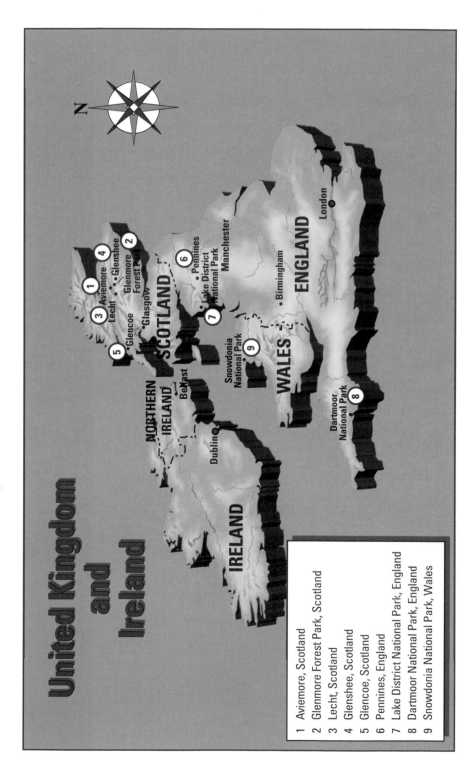

United Kingdom and Ireland

1 Aviemore, Scotland
2 Glenmore Forest Park, Scotland
3 Lecht, Scotland
4 Glenshee, Scotland
5 Glencoe, Scotland
6 Pennines, England
7 Lake District National Park, England
8 Dartmoor National Park, England
9 Snowdonia National Park, Wales

National Park in the northwest retain their snowfall for at least a month or two each year on average. In the southwest, **Dartmoor National Park** regularly gets a few weeks of snow, but you may be rather far from assistance here, if it is needed. You may be hard pressed at any of these locales to find snowshoe or ski supplies, however, so you should be equipped before you head out.

Snowdonia National Park in Wales is also a good place to look for snow, although there is not an extensive support structure (resorts, suppliers, etc.) here.

© Windrush Photos/Frank V Blackburn

You may have to search for snow in the U.K., but when you find it you'll be rewarded.

Western Europe by Snowshoe

There are two primary snow areas in western Europe. The first is the far north: Iceland, Norway, Sweden, and Finland all get a good deal of snow, to put it lightly. The other area is the Alps. Stretching from France to Austria, to snowshoers the Alps are a wintry haven in otherwise temperate climes.

FRANCE

Long known as the world capital of alpinism, the Bois du Bouchet forest paths near **Chamonix** provide snowshoers trails with a park-like setting. The trails start at the Sports Center and extend through 12 kilometers (7.5 miles) of undulating landscape. Even more vigorous is the 25K (15.5-mile) trip toward Le Lavancher and Les Grands Montets to Argentiere and back to the Sports Center. The trails pass through small villas and hamlets, with their accompanying small cafés, where you may find your fill of sights and refreshments. Write: Tourist Office, 74400 Chamonix, France; or phone 50-53-0214.

© Chamonix/Mont-Blanc, France

Vallée Blanche in the Chamonix region.

European Destinations

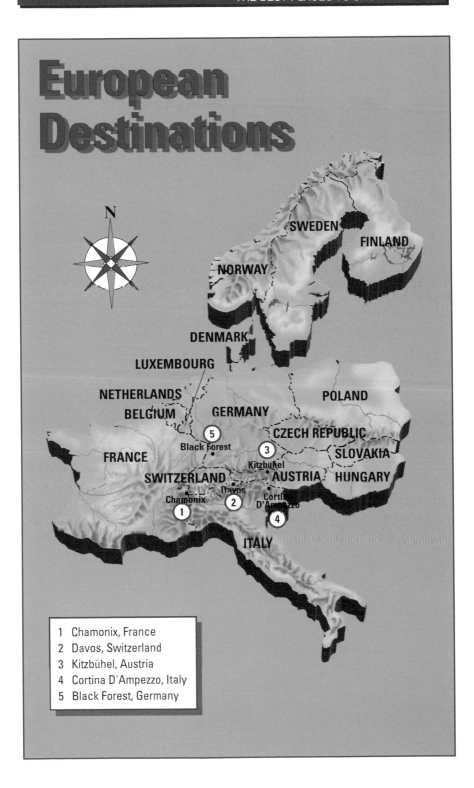

1 Chamonix, France
2 Davos, Switzerland
3 Kitzbühel, Austria
4 Cortina D'Ampezzo, Italy
5 Black Forest, Germany

SWITZERLAND

Davos is one of Switzerland's premier snow play areas. The trail system has about 80 kilometers (50 miles) of prepared trails through the town, around the lake in Davos Dorf, and circling up the beautifully wooded side valleys. The uphill climbs guarantee frequent stops for fluid replacement, but if you find yourself too sapped to go on, buses return regularly from all the valleys to Davos. If this isn't enough, night snowshoeing is yours on a nearby floodlit track. Write: Davos Tourist Office, CH 7270 Davos Platz, Switzerland; or phone Langlauf-Zentrum (Cross-Country Center) at 41-083-5-44-55.

AUSTRIA

The medieval walled city of **Kitzbühel** is distinguished by long and forested valleys ideal for snowshoers. The area maintains a permanent trail system with distances between 3 and 13 kilometers (2–8 miles) that challenge all levels of snowshoers. A must-try trail begins near the base of the Hahnenkamm at Maurachfeld. This 14K (9-mile) trail on the Pass Thurn side of Kitzbühel follows the river past several roadside inns to the Gasthaus Hechenmoos, a popular local gathering place. Write: The Tourist Office, Hinterstadt 18, A-6370, Kitzbühel, Austria; or phone 43-5356-21-55.

ITALY

Considered Italy's most glamorous resort area, **Cortina d'Ampezzo** became well known after the 1956 Winter Olympic Games, but its short season—mid-December through early April—limits its attraction for some. With 52 cable cars and lifts, 20 mountain restaurants, and altitudes as high as 2,800 meters (9,184 ft), there's plenty of terrain to explore. A cross-country ski school (Scuola di Sci per Fondo) north of town provides well-planned routes for snowshoers and Nordic aficionados. The trails are marked and you can get information at the tourist office or the school about trips into the back country. If you snowshoe into the deep woods, the only visible signs of life might be the tracks of mountain goat and ermine. Write: Azienda Promozione Turistica, Piazetta S. Francesco, 832043 Cortina d'Ampezzo, Italy; or phone 39-436-3231.

GERMANY

With 965 kilometers (600 miles) of cross-country trails to choose from, the **Black Forest** region of Germany is ideal for the sport snowshoer. Some of the best areas are around Titisee and up the slopes to the Feldberg, the tallest mountain in the region. Many of the trails take you through charming countryside with guesthouses and hotels along the way. This is Germany's best-known cross-country ski area, and the people extend a warm invitation to snowshoers to join them. Write: German National Tourist Offices, 122 E. 42nd St., 52nd Floor, New York, NY 10168; or phone 212-661-7200.

Scenic Australia and New Zealand

With nearly half the continent in the tropics, snowshoeing in Australia is somewhat hampered by lack of snow. There are some Australian areas that receive snowfall, however, and many think the abundant winter snow of New Zealand more than compensates for the meager output of its neighbor.

AUSTRALIA

Although snowshoeing is not yet widely popular in Australia, the increasing variety of snow sports offered here seems to indicate that it won't be long before snowshoeing catches on.

Snowshoers in Australia would do well to consider a few details: The first is that the snow season in Australia is short, running only from July through early September. The second is that using ski resorts can be expensive—lift tickets average $45 or more, and accommodations are likewise pricey in the resort areas. The third is that you need to call ahead to make sure snowshoeing is allowed on a particular resort's trails.

Also know that there is only one main Australian region with significant snowfall: the **Snowy Mountains**. This range straddles the border between Victoria and New South Wales and contains the continent's highest peaks. The Snowy Mountains are part of Australia's Great Dividing Range and lie within Kosciusko National Park.

Thredbo Village is located at the bottom of Mt. Crackenback, one of the longest downhills in the country. Thredbo's ski runs are more heavily forested than those of its competitors, which makes this resort one of the most popular in Australia. Though Australian snowfall can be quite unpredictable (many compare the Australian snow season to that of the northeastern United States), at Thredbo the upper half of the mountain usually has great snow and huge snowfields that stretch for miles, making their runs bigger than many in Switzerland. In all, there are 64 kilometers (40 miles) of trails at Thredbo. Phone the Thredbo Resort Centre at 064 57-6360 or Thredbo Snow Reports at 064 57-4011.

When the weather is hospitable and the snow plentiful, we recommend a snowshoe adventure to the top of **Mt. Kosciusko**. At 2,228 meters (7,310 ft) it's the highest peak in Australia. If you're feeling particularly energetic you can snowshoe up, but most people take the Mt. Crackenback chairlift to the top. From the top of the lift you can snowshoe to the summit over a fairly easy 3K (1.8-mile) trail. The view from the top of this peak is well worth the effort. Phone Kosciusko National Park Visitors Centre at 064 56-2102.

Although **Smiggins Hole** and **Perisher Valley** are two separate ski

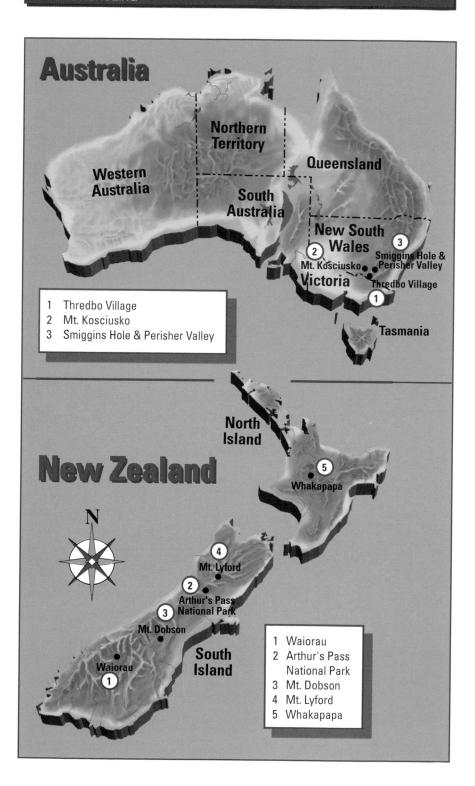

Australia

Northern Territory

Western Australia

Queensland

South Australia

New South Wales

Smiggins Hole & Perisher Valley

Mt. Kosciusko

Victoria

Thredbo Village

Tasmania

1 Thredbo Village
2 Mt. Kosciusko
3 Smiggins Hole & Perisher Valley

New Zealand

North Island

Whakapapa

N

Mt. Lyford

Arthur's Pass National Park

Mt. Dobson

South Island

Waiorau

1 Waiorau
2 Arthur's Pass National Park
3 Mt. Dobson
4 Mt. Lyford
5 Whakapapa

resorts, most people speak of them interchangeably, as you can buy one lift ticket and ski both. With over 30 ski lifts between them, they together comprise the largest ski area in Australia. In Perisher Valley, we recommend trying the Charlotte Pass area, recently popular in Australia for its ski touring country. This is the highest and one of the oldest and most remote of Australia's ski resorts. If you are adventurous and ready for a challenge, snowshoes are ideal in this environment. One challenge is to snowshoe the trail from Charlotte Pass to Thredbo.

NEW ZEALAND

Many Australians now come to New Zealand to engage in winter sports. Thanks to New Zealand's more temperate latitudes and higher mountains, the season here is longer (from June through as late as mid-November, depending on the area) and more predictable, the costs are lower, and there are more choices of places to go.

The only commercial Nordic area in New Zealand, **Waiorau** stands out as a snowshoeing destination. Here are 25 kilometers (15.5 miles) of groomed trails and, more important for the snowshoer, a vast rolling, snow-covered countryside. Located 26 kilometers (16 miles) from Wanaka on the Pisa Range, high above Lake Wanaka, this area offers incredible views of the surrounding lands. The season runs from late June through late September. Phone 03 443-7542 or 03 443-7544.

© Kawaru Rafts, New Zealand

New Zealand's high mountains extend the snowshoeing season.

Just a few hours' drive from Christchurch, **Arthur's Pass National Park** serves as the gateway to the West Coast of New Zealand. The park has a hostel, service station, huts for several mountain clubs, and serves as the starting point for climbing and snowshoeing into the Southern Alps. This is a gentle mountainous area with long valleys, well-maintained huts, and clearly marked trails. Hopping between passes from one valley to another is possible, but rigorous, as snow lies deep enough on all the Main Divide passes to make crossing them exhausting. A day trip from the road will provide a wide range of alternatives—leaving at dawn from a base at Arthur's Pass village should allow you enough time to snowshoe up to Temple Basin.

If you're looking for incredible scenery, try **Mt. Dobson**, 26 kilometers (16 miles) from Fairlie. Snowshoeing to the summit of Mt. Dobson will exhilarate you, and the views from the top are breathtaking. On a clear day you can see Mt. Cook, the Pacific Ocean, and the Southern Alps. Phone 03 685-8039.

The newest commercial ski area in New Zealand is **Mt. Lyford** in North Canterbury, 75 kilometers (47 miles) from Hanmer Springs. Built in conjunction with a wilderness retreat, Lyford offers an idyllic combination of winter sports, including cross-country skiing, ice skating, and hot springs. Its 15 kilometers (9 miles) of groomed cross-country trails are not extensive, but a snowshoer is not limited to those. Phone 03 343-0248.

Located on the North Island and offering the largest area of groomed trails in New Zealand is **Whakapapa** in the Tongariro National Park. Snow is good here from June through mid-November. Phone 07 892-3738.

Limitless Adventure

Don't think your travels are limited to the places we have listed. Seek out your own ideal snowshoeing destinations, or just find them along the way. If you take your snowshoes with you when you travel, you'll always be prepared to take advantage of your surroundings and explore the land around you, whatever the weather. Remember, somewhere around the world it's snowing, so the only limits to your snowshoeing travels are those of your imagination.

6

PURSUING SNOW- SHOEING FURTHER

Are you equipped? Are you physically fit? Are you familiar with the basic snowshoeing moves and the health and safety issues that go along with snowshoeing? If you can answer "yes" to these questions, you are ready to pursue snowshoeing further.

If you are athletic, or aspire to be athletic, you may want to take up snowshoe running—it's easy on the body and can be a welcome alternative to other, more traditional workouts. Those who want a more relaxing option for their weekend outings may want to take up the art of tracking; observing the signs of wildlife is easier in the winter, and snowshoes are the ideal way to position yourself for some great viewing.

The list of options for the experienced snowshoer is open-ended. From the traditional—winter backpacking, camping, and mountain climbing—to the modern or just plain silly—snowshoe ultimate Frisbee and snowshoe poker—we've done just about everything on snowshoes that we could have done on warm, dry ground.

Running

People have been running and racing on snowshoes for a long time, but recently snowshoe running has grown rapidly in popularity. Today, snowshoes are designed specifically for racing, and more and more shoers want the special pleasures and aerobic benefits that running has to offer.

Running on snowshoes takes only slightly more thought than running on the roads or trails. For most runners, snowshoe running will be an absolute joy and wonder. You have freedom to go wherever you want, up and down any slope, at whatever pace you choose, and the variety snowrunning offers might make you look at your current running regimen in a whole new light.

© John Kelly

Snowshoes give you the freedom to run on top of the snow.

SAFETY TIP Don't consider starting snowshoe running unless you are comfortable both with running on dry land and handling the basic snowshoe moves.

As for technique, it is important to try to run smoothly and develop a rhythm in your stride at a constant intensity level. You also need to concentrate on your footing, because the amount of traction you have can vary quickly and dramatically. Lightly packed snow is the best surface for snowshoe running, as breaking trail increases the work load and energy costs by about 50%.

Economy of movement will lower your work load and enhance your performance. To become efficient, use the least amount of leg lift required

© Teri Henderson

Efficient snowrunning technique can lower your times and decrease wasted energy.

to raise the shoe out of the snow and keep your feet as close together as you can. If you have ever run in hard-packed sand and looked back at your path, you will see that your footprints form a straight line. That's because when you are running your footplant is directly under your body's center. Try the same when snowshoeing—you want as little outswing and waddling as possible. Asymmetrically shaped snowshoes will help in this regard.

Regular runners will notice a difference in stress points while snowshoeing. When running uphill, the calf muscle is shortened when you wear snowshoes because the heel doesn't land. Also, most runners require tremendous hamstring strength, as this is the muscle group that drives the leg forward. In contrast, snowshoe runners recruit their quads and hamstrings, the quads being key in lifting the extra weight of the snowshoe out of the snow.

For your first snowshoe run, start on a flat trail and go slowly as you adjust to the balance and coordination skills required. Most find that on packed surfaces, snowshoe running requires about 2 extra minutes per mile to be added to your 10K (6.2-mile) running time if you are a sub 40-minute racer, or 3 minutes added if you are above 40 minutes for a 10K. This means that snowshoe running has roughly a 25% to 35% increase in energy cost compared to running without snowshoes. For an experiment, compare your times on one of your usual running courses in normal conditions wearing running shoes with your times in the winter wearing snowshoes.

TRAIL TIP   We all—shoers, skiers, and snowmobilers—need to share trails with mutual respect. When snowshoeing on Nordic ski trails, take care to stay out of the diagonal tracks groomed on the skating trail area.

Dedicating a pair of running flats to your racing snowshoes is optimal and will enhance your performance and comfort. For most models and manufacturers, you must jerry-rig a way to attach the racing flats permanently to your snowshoe pivot system. Some manufacturers have models that allow direct mounting of your running shoes. Others require you to disassemble and remove the binding. With a drill, make holes through the midsoles and outersoles at the exact location where the existing fastening screws are placed, then fasten your shoes right there to the pivot system. Place a plastic or thick innersole over the flathead screws so you don't feel them. (*Note.* This direct attachment system does not work on all snowshoe models.)

Dress appropriately for your workouts. Usually this means dressing exactly as you would going for a run. A fanny pack can be handy to carry wind pants and a jacket in case the temperature changes. Two layers are usually adequate: a ventilation layer of tights and long-sleeve, pull-push fabric top and a thermal layer of pile. You'll usually remove the thermal layer after you have warmed up.

Carry your hydration pack or water bottles. On an out-and-back course, you might stash a water bottle or two for later retrieval. You will definitely need to pace yourself because of the increased work load; it's easy to reach your anaerobic heart rate threshold quickly if you don't. If necessary, wear your heart rate monitor to hold you back from training in the upper zones. Snowshoe running can really make you work.

COMMON SNOWSHOE RUNNING ERRORS

You can avoid some common problems early in your snowshoe running career by following the guidelines given to solve these problems:

- *Knees too high:* For maximum economy of movement, keep to a shuffling gait with knees low.

- *Stride too wide:* Again, for efficiency and comfort, try to keep your feet as close together as you can.

- *Toe-first foot plant:* By landing on your forefoot rather than the heel, you strain your calf muscles. Keep your heels down just as when running on the roads.

- *Foot pain:* Beginners often tighten the binding so much that they bruise the top of their forefoot—that's just not necessary.

- *Nicked ankles:* Because of the width of snowshoes, it is common for snowshoe runners to nick the insides of their ankles, which in shoers' lingo is called "drawing blood." The best prevention is to lightly outkick as your foot swings forward or to use asymmetrical snowshoes. Usually, the forward medial portion of the toe is what strikes the ankle, especially if the shoe does not track straight.

Racing

Snowshoe racing at this point has regional characteristics. Multisport races such as winter duathlons, triathlons, and quadrathlons are popular in the western United States. Hillclimbs and untracked, trail-breaking and bushwhacking courses are prevalent in the Rockies. Prepared courses, often snow-covered running tracks, are popular in the eastern United States and Canada.

Duathlons and triathlons are increasing in popularity, with other winter sports such as Nordic skiing, ice skating, or mountain biking being combined with snowshoeing. For these events, quick-release bindings in the snowshoes have been designed using bungee cord–type heel straps.

© Carl Heilman II

Snowshoe racing allows you to experience the thrill of competition.

The snowshoe racing community is currently struggling with regulations for the sport. Issues such as the minimum size of the snowshoe and the type of racecourse venue are hot discussion topics. However, it is important to remember that a snowshoe's basic purpose is to provide flotation over snow. If a racecourse is designed in such a way as to encourage those competitors whose snowshoes provide good flotation, then the issue of snowshoe size is eliminated. If a race director plots a racecourse that is so hard-packed that one might as easily race in a pair of running shoes alone, then the course is the problem.

As snowshoe running and racing have grown, governing bodies such as the Canadian Snowshoe Union have tried to organize and standardize the sport. Among the goals of these groups is to preserve the tradition of wooden snowshoes by recommending separate divisions for traditional and sport snowshoes. They are also trying to set rules standardizing snowshoe frame geometry.

Some snowshoe runners believe that the sport should remain as it is, without standardization. Those who disagree believe that standardization of equipment, distances, and rules is a must for fair competition. Either way, these issues are far from settled, and individual input can really make a difference at this formative stage in the evolution of snowshoe running and racing.

Camping and Mountaineering

If you are the rugged type who wants to get away from it all, winter camping and mountaineering are for you. There is no time like the winter to explore the wild and scenic outdoors, and sometimes just going out for day hikes can get pretty limiting.

However, there are serious trade-offs for the luxury of going where others aren't and staying out longer; this is not a pastime to be taken lightly. If you think you are a competent camper and outdoorsperson in the summer, that's a good start, but it's only part of what you need to head out into the snow for extended periods of time.

Safety becomes paramount. At least one and preferably two members of your party should know first aid, including avalanche rescue techniques. Setting out on a whim with just a friend or two has become a thing of the past. Being a successful winter camper and mountaineer also means being a thorough planner, and the more knowledgeable companions you have going out there with you, the better.

The list of gear you will need to take expands seemingly geometrically, because unlike the day shoer, you need to provide for warmth, food, *and* shelter. You should refer to technical books on your topic (back-country camping, ice climbing, etc.) for complete descriptions of your gear needs, because they are extensive and very specific.

For starters, you'll want a long-handled ice ax, not ski or snowshoe poles. You will also need a short technical ax for ice climbing and a long-handled ax for snowshoeing. You can retrofit one end of a long-handled ax with a ski pole basket to make it more useful, but make sure you can easily take the basket on and off.

Regarding clothing, once you start winter camping and mountaineering, you enter the true three-layer group; layers for ventilation, insulation, and water/wind resistance are imperative. And there are trade-offs in how you

© Dugald Bremner

Snowshoes make winter camping and exploring easier and more enjoyable.

gear up. The trade-off here is cost in weight versus cost in cash. The more apparel and gear and the more beefy your footwear, the more the cost in work load. Of course, cutting-edge equipment and clothing get lighter and lighter each year, but there is the other cost—financial. It is best to experiment until you find a combination that works in different weather conditions and doesn't require you to carry too much weight or spend too much money.

Tracking

If you like taking your outings at a slower pace, tracking is for you. This is an activity that rewards the patient and the careful but still can be an exciting way to spend a day in the winter outdoors.

Basically, tracking is about *seeing*—opening up your senses to the broader environment you enter in the snow-covered wilds. If you've watched a deer or a rabbit in the wild, you can sense how attuned they are to their environment. They are constantly putting their noses to the wind, flicking their ears in all directions to pick up sounds, and darting their eyes to pick up movement. These animals are completely involved in the constant checking of all their senses. And we humans? We are so involved in our urban experiences and removed from issues of day-to-day survival that we've forgotten how to watch and listen.

We suggest that you make the most of the time you spend in the wild by making use of all your senses. Seeing the wild world attentively may take a little knowledge, practice, and care, but it can be very rewarding.

© Carl Heilman II

The more you learn about tracking, the more fun it becomes.

Equipping yourself with some information beforehand, such as learning the tracks of a few common animals, is a valuable first step. A light snow; a calm, sunny day; and a trail are all you need to get started. To understand an animal and its life you should not merely identify its tracks but also follow the prints for a distance. As you do, you notice the changes in the tracks—the distance between leaps or steps, the pauses for food. Try to determine why the animal may have bolted off quickly or paused. Are there other tracks nearby? Was this animal hunting, or being hunted? What stories may have been played out here? Such questions are often easier answered on a snow trail in the winter than on a dusty path in the summer.

EARTH WATCH

There is a big difference between respectfully observing or photographing an animal from a distance and carelessly intruding into its home and disturbing its breeding, feeding, or resting patterns. Keep your distance!

When tracking through the winter snowfields, you may want to bring a small pair of binoculars, a spiral notebook, a pen, and a ruler. If you want to record the trails you find, you might also bring a camera equipped with a good polarizing filter. The ruler and pad come in handy if you're not sure about your identification of the tracks and need to make some notes on the size of the print or rough drawings for more thorough investigation when you get back home.

Being a Snowshoer

We have been told that one of the cultural and political imperatives in Japan today is *watch-do-be*. For example, many enjoy *watching* sporting events but still know it is better to *do* them. The final stage, to *be*, is not only a Japanese goal but can be ours as well.

This past year Sally raced in her first winter multisport race—the Mt. Taylor Quadrathlon. The four-sport event started at 6,000 feet (1,829 m) and finished at the top of New Mexico's Mt. Taylor at an elevation of 11,000 feet (3,353 m).

The race started at a warm 36° Fahrenheit (2.2 °C). The first leg was a 13-mile (21-km) bike ride, ascending 1,500 feet (457 m) and leading into a 5-mile (8-km) snowshoe run, with another 1,500-foot (457-m) gain in elevation. At the completion of the run, snow began to fall and the winds started to gust. Donning cross-country skis, the competitors climbed another 1,500 feet (457 m) in 2.5 miles (4 km). At the final transition it was clear how cold it was when the cups of water volunteers passed out had already turned to ice.

At the top of Mt. Taylor flags whipped with loud cracks as the winds gusted at over 30 miles (48 km) per hour. Food and drinks were offered, but the only thought on the competitors' minds was to get off this mountain. The descent was the same as the ascent, with no relief from wind or snow during any of the four legs over the entire 21-mile (34-km) return.

One wonders why 600 athletes would forge the altitude, the cold, the wind, the distance, the hours, the high heart rates, the fatigue, and the

© R. Bossi

Watching and doing are good first steps, but *being* a snowshoer is the ultimate.

hardship when they could have spent their Saturday morning watching the race (or the television) instead. Surely the occasional shoers, cyclists, and runners, who may enjoy their hobby only when it is comfortable, would never have set foot upon the mountain that day.

How did Sally get to the finish line? And, more importantly, why was she there? We think it's because we have gone past watching and doing and have come to *be*. We are now explorers of the winter landscape who, with physical training and reliable equipment, know only the bounds of our imaginations. We have come to be snowshoers. We hope you become snowshoers, too.

APPENDIX

FOR MORE INFORMATION

Organizations

There is currently only one active, large-scale snowshoeing organization. You may contact them for details on membership, races, etc.

International Amateur Snowshoe Racing Federation
Canadian Snowshoe Association
9 Beriault
Hull, Québec, J8X 1A1, Canada

Other Reading

Cross-Country Skiing and Snowshoeing by Erwin A. Bauer
Winchester Press, New York, 1975.

The Snowshoe Book by William Osgood and Leslie Hurley
The Stephen Greene Press, Lexington, MA, 1971.

Snowshoeing by Gene Prater
The Mountaineers, Seattle, 1988.

Walk into Winter: A Complete Snowshoeing and Winter Camping Guide by
   Gerry Wolfram
Charles Scribner's Sons, New York, 1977.

Snowshoe Manufacturers

Companies that distribute their snowshoes on a regional or national level through retailers or distributors are listed here. It is impossible to give prices, models, or other specific information because product lines are always changing. Please contact the manufacturer directly for current information.

Sport Snowshoes

Atlas Snowshoe Company
81 Lafayette Street
San Francisco, CA 94103
415-703-0414

Belle Chase Snowshoes
IEL Limited
P.O. Box 340
St-Damien, Quebec
Canada G0R 2Y0
418-789-2585
   Note. Plastic snowshoes only.

Good Thunder Snowshoes
3945 Aldrich Avenue South
Minneapolis, MN 55409
612-824-2385

Northern Lites
1300 Cleveland Avenue
Wausau, WI 54401
800-360-LITE

Prater Snowshoes
1201 North A Street
Ellensburg, WA 98926
509-962-1864

Redfeather Snowshoes
1280 Ute Avenue, #20
Aspen, CO 81611
800-525-0081

YubaShoes Sport Snowshoes
2412 J Street
Sacramento, CA 95816
800-598-YUBA or 916-441-6300

Traditional Snowshoes

Attikamek Snowshoe
The Trust for Native American Cultures and Crafts
Box 142
Greenville, NH 03048
603-878-2944
   Note. This is a nonprofit foundation engaged in the documentation of the
traditional technologies and survival skills of the northern Native Americans.

Avery and Sons
P.O. Box 339, Paradise Road
Whitney, Ontario
Canada K0J 2M0
613-637-2825

Cole Alpine Manufacturing
6114 164th Avenue S.E.
Issaquah, WA 98027
206-746-2230

Faber Safesport Snowshoe Company
P.O. Box 100
Loretteville, Quebec
Canada G2B 3W6
418-842-8476

Green's Custom Snow Shoes
R.D. 1
Broadlibin, NY 12025
518-883-3703

Havlick Snowshoe Company
2513 State Highway 30, Drawer QQ
Mayfield, NY 12117
518-661-6447

Iverson Snowshoe Company
P.O. Box 85
Shingleton, MI 49884
906-452-6370

Raquettes Aigle Noir, Inc.
251, Boulevard La Riviere
CP 250 Loretteville, Quebec
Canada G2A 1H2
418-842-4045

Sherpa Outdoor Products
444 S. Pine Street
Burlington, WI 53105
800-621-2277

Stowe Snowshoe Company (Tubbs)
P.O. Box 207
Stowe, VT 05672
802-253-7398

Mountaineer Snowshoes

Ramer Products, Ltd.
1803 South Foothills Highway
Boulder, CO 80303-7466
303-499-4466

Snowshoe Kits

Wilcox and Williams Kits
6105 Halifax Avenue
Edina, MN 55424
612-929-4935

SNOWSHOEING LINGO

age hardening—Snow that has been on the ground long enough will condense and pack. In areas like British Columbia, this process may occur after only 20 to 30 minutes on the ground. Age-hardened snow is also called "consolidated snow."

Alaskan—An elongated, teardrop-shaped snowshoe frame. Also called the "Yukon," "Pickerel," "cross-country," or "trail" snowshoe.

Algonquin—A wide, teardrop-shaped snowshoe frame. Also known as the "Maine," "Michigan," or "beavertail."

anorak—An outer-layer jacket for cold weather, usually a pullover-style windbreaker.

ball-joint fatigue—Walking or running with a waddle or straddle stance (such as that caused by especially wide snowshoes) places the leg at an unnatural angle. This stresses the hip joint and tendons rapidly, especially when the extra weight of snowshoes and gear are factored in.

bare-boot—When the snow is hard and crusty, you can make better progress, especially by kick-stepping, without snowshoes on, instead of wearing just your "bare boots."

bearpaw—The original round and wide snowshoe frame geometry.

beavertail—A wide, teardrop-shaped snowshoe frame. Also known as the "Maine," "Michigan," or "Algonquin."

binding—The part of a snowshoe that attaches to the footwear. In traditional snowshoes, bindings are often called "riggings." Bindings come in such designs as the "H" and the "A," so-called because of their shape.

booties—Usually made from neoprene or lightweight nylon, these are used to cover non–boot-type shoes to keep them warm and dry.

breaking trail—The task of the lead snowshoer, who steps or stomps through the snow to make a solid path for others to follow.

bushwhack course—This is a type of snowshoe course designed to be off-trail and to cut through untracked snow and bushes. Such a course is in sharp contrast to the groomed and packed snowshoe trails usually found at Nordic resorts.

carrying surface—The surface area of a snowshoe; the larger the surface area, the more flotation and support for the snowshoer.

claw—Like a crampon but with comparatively short serrations. Claws are an angle traction device attached to sport snowshoes. They give a "grip" comparable to that provided by the webbing of traditional snowshoes and are used in conditions where ice or steep surfaces are not encountered.

crampon—Generally made from heat-treated aluminum or tempered carbon steel, this traction device may be attached to a snowshoe's pivot rod to prevent slippage. Crampons or "cramps" are particularly necessary in conditions where ice or steep terrain is common.

decking—The solid piece of rubber-like material attached to the bottom of a snowshoe frame that provides flotation for the snowshoer. Most sport snowshoe decks are made of Hypalon and attached with aluminum rivets. In traditional snowshoes, decking is known as "webbing" and is attached with synthetic or rawhide lacing.

double step—A snowshoe technique in which you stamp down with about 50% of your weight on the forward snowshoe and hesitate for a second. During this split second, the snow consolidates or "age hardens," firming up for added flotation.

drawing blood—Nicking the insides of your ankles with your snowshoes. This is a more common problem with symmetrical or especially wide shoes.

duathlon—A competitive sport including two activities. For example, a winter duathlon might consist of a snowshoeing/cross-country skiing or ice skating/snowshoeing combination.

fall line—The shortest distance down a slope. The direction perpendicular to the ground, which an object (you, a rock, snow) would fall.

flotation—The amount of loft provided by snowshoes. The more the flotation the better because you will sink less into the snow.

frame geometry—The size and shape of a snowshoe frame.

glissade—A controlled glide.

heel straps—The part of the snowshoe binding that secures the heel. It is a strap that wraps around the back of the shoer's footwear.

hoarfrost—The white, ice-like frost that collects on the outside of your garments as released perspiration freezes to the exterior of your clothing. "Depth hoar" is crystalline, nonpacking frost that forms beneath the snow's surface during long periods of extreme subzero temperatures; it can be highly unstable.

Hypalon—A rubberized synthetic decking material made by DuPont that whitewater rafts, snowshoe decks, parts of athletic shoes, and other items are made from. It doesn't stain, it is resistant to ultraviolet rays that can cause fading or fabric decay, and when punctured or cut it resists further tearing.

kick-stepping—A snowshoe technique used for climbing straight uphill. You stamp the shoe and crampon hard into the snow perpendicular to the fall line, creating a "step" for the next shoer.

lacing—Same as webbing.

Leatherman—A backpacker's tool that includes a screwdriver, saw, awl, pliers, knives, and more; it is very useful if you need to repair your gear in an emergency.

Loft—Insulated padding for warmth, as in a sleeping bag.

Maine—A wide, teardrop-shaped snowshoe frame. Also known as the "Michigan," "Algonquin," or "beavertail."

master cord—Found in traditional snowshoes, it is the heavy cording in the rear of the toe hole that supports the bindings.

Michigan—A wide, teardrop-shaped snowshoe frame. Also known as the "Maine," "Algonquin," or "beavertail."

Ojibwa—A snowshoe frame with pointed toe and tail.

Pickerel—An elongated, teardrop-shaped snowshoe frame. Also called the "Yukon," "Alaskan," "cross-country," or "trail" snowshoe.

pivot rod/bar—Usually made of a solid material such as aluminum, this rod attaches to the frame and allows the foot and binding to rotate as the snowshoer moves forward. Some pivot systems are made from rubberized material with elastic properties. In traditional snowshoeing, this is known as the "cross member forward."

points—The sharp and sturdy spikes or teeth on a crampon or claw used for traction, especially when climbing. Also called spikes.

post-holing—Sinking into the snow when taking steps. The opposite of flotation.

pulk—A small snow sled pulled by snowshoers, skiers, mushers (dog sledders), reindeer (mostly in Scandinavia), and runners. Pulks are made from wood or fiberglass and come in several shapes and sizes.

shoeing—The act of snowshoeing.

shoer—Anyone who snowshoes.

shuffle-step—Snowshoe running style in which you take the weight off the snowshoe and shuffle it ahead. Used only on well-packed trails over moderately sloping terrain, this stride is best used for long-distance snowshoe runs or tramps.

snowpoles—Distinguished from ski poles by their oversized baskets, snowpoles are used for stability, provide an upper body workout, and can be converted into an avalanche probe for safety.

snowshoe sliding—A downhill technique similar to a glissade, with the snowshoes acting as modified skis. The feet may take either a parallel or diagonal stance.

tail—The rear area of a snowshoe. There are curved, pointed, short, and long tail shapes. In the past, the tail served as a sort of rudder; dragging it helped keep the shoe pointed straight ahead.

toe hole—The opening in the front decking that allows the forefoot to pivot through a complete range of motion.

trail treader—In a single line of snowshoers this is the rear or "whipper-in" position.

tramp—A recreational snowshoe event begun in the mid-1800s as a winter outing or cross-country workout.

traversing—A snowshoe technique in which the shoer kicks the snowshoe sideways into a slope, moving diagonally across the slope's face. Also, stepping sideways into the slope and stamping down, thereby forcing the edge of the snowshoe into the slope. This technique is not recommended because of the snowshoes' lack of lateral traction.

tuque—A knitted hat adorned with a tassel on the top, the traditional headgear for snowshoers.

webbed feet—A nickname for snowshoers. A web is another term for a traditional snowshoe.

webbing—The interwoven decking that serves as the carrying surface for traditional snowshoes, usually made of rawhide or neoprene.

Westerns—The original small, light-weight, modern snowshoes first developed in the early 1950s. Made from aircraft-quality aluminum with a solid neoprene/nylon decking laced to the frame.

Westover—A snowshoe frame with a stubby, squared-off tail, named for its designer, Floyd Westover of Meco, Vermont, who pioneered not only its frame geometry but also the use of nylon-reinforced neoprene webbing.

Yukon—An elongated, teardrop-shaped snowshoe frame. Also called the "Pickerel," "Alaskan," "cross-country," or "trail" snowshoe.

INDEX

ABOUT THE AUTHORS

Melissa McKenzie and Sally Edwards

Sally Edwards and Melissa McKenzie, both avid snowshoers, are the cofounders of YubaShoes Sport Snowshoes, a manufacturing company of high-performance snowshoes.

Edwards has been committed to fitness all her life. One of the founders of triathlon competition, she has completed 13 Ironman triathlons, finishing in the top five in the master's or open division in each. She competed in the 1984 Olympic Marathon Trials and set the women's record at the 1993 Iditashoe 100-Mile Snowshoe Race in Alaska with a time of 24 hours, 1 minute. She has won dozens of other endurance events, including the master's division of the 1994 Mt. Taylor Quadrathlon, a combination of snowshoeing, cross-country skiing, running, and cycling.

In addition to *Snowshoeing*, Edwards has written 7 books on sports, fitness, and diet and more than 300 magazine and newspaper articles. She is a well-known professional speaker and the national spokesperson for the Danskin Women's Triathlon Series since 1990. One of the founders of Triathlon Federation/USA, she served as its vice president for seven years.

Edwards earned her master's degree in exercise physiology from the University of California at Berkeley, in 1970 and her MBA from National University in 1986.

Melissa McKenzie left her job as a marketing executive for a cellular telephone company to launch YubaShoes with Sally Edwards. Having earned her MBA from Boston University in 1986, McKenzie was no stranger to the corporate environment. YubaShoes became her first entrepreneurial venture, allowing her to combine vocation and avocation.

McKenzie's lifelong interest in the outdoors and her bachelor's degree in biology, with an emphasis on botany and ecology, allowed her to make major contributions to the chapters in this book that focus on nature. A member of the Sierra Club and the National Audubon Society, McKenzie hopes to inspire others to become more familiar with the great outdoors.

Acknowledgments

To Donna Lee, for her artistry and craftsmanship. Without her, this book would be a lesser thing.

We also owe thanks to our sidebar contributors:

Marty Maskall is the editor of *The Attitude Treasury: 101 Inspiring Quotations* and *The Athena Treasury: 101 Inspiring Quotations by Women.* Contact her at P.O. Box 1765, Fair Oaks, CA 95628.

John Browning owns *Wilderness Connection*, an outdoor specialty store in Mequon, Wisconsin and is an expert on traditional snowshoes. He can be reached at 6077 W. Mequon Rd., Mequon, WI 53092. We're grateful for his assistance in our discussion of the various traditional snowshoe models.

Carl Heilman II, known for his hand-crafted mountaineering and recreational snowshoes, has been an avid snowshoer since making his first pair in 1974. As New York State licensed guides, he and his wife have been leading snowshoeing workshops since 1985. Contact him at Route 8, RR1, Box 213A, Brant Lake, NY 12815.

Herb Lindsey, former American 10,000-meter record holder, challenged the best to win the overall men's division at the 1993 Mt. Hood Snowshoe Race. Write him at P.O. Box 767, Washburn, WI 54891.

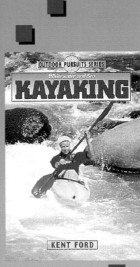

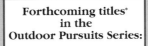